TPM
THAT WORKS

The Theory and Design of
Total Productive Maintenance

A Guide for Implementing TPM

Bill N. Maggard, P.E.

TPM Press, Inc.
Pittsburgh, Pennsylvania   Charlotte, North Carolina

TPM Press, Inc.
4018 Letort Lane
Allison Park, PA 15101, USA
Phone: (412) 486-6340
Fax: (412) 486-6375

Library of Congress Catalog Card Number: 92-41792
ISBN: 1-882258-01-0

Printed and bound by Jostens Winston-Salem

Printed in the United States of America

Library of Congress Cataloging-in-Publication Data

Maggard, Bill N.
  TPM that Works / Bill N. Maggard
  Includes index.
  1. Total productive maintenance 2. Plant maintenance
  I. Title.
  TS192.M29 1992   658.2'02--dc20   92-41792
  ISBN 1-882258-01-0   CIP

10 9 8 7 6 5 4 3

Table of Contents

Acknowledgments

The development of the TPM program at Tennessee Eastman involved the expenditure of thousands of hours by hundreds of people. They all contributed to this book -- some by participating in the program, some by preparing the actual documentation, and some by giving constant support in both hours and dollars. In particular, I would like to acknowledge the invaluable help of the following:

-- All the initial TPM Pilot Teams at Tennessee Eastman. With great commitment, they enthusiastically supported TPM's implementation; they also helped with the survey which addressed the social issues of TPM. Their many suggestions and recommendations have contributed significantly to the improvements in the deployment process.

-- All the teams that have been active in implementing and steering TPM throughout Tennessee Eastman.

-- Aubrey Daniels and Associates of Tucker, Georgia, for their contribution to the Performance Management portion of TPM and for their guidance in teaching us how to persuade people to make decisions or take actions based on their own judgment.

-- Charlie Bailey, previously Superintendent of Plant Maintenance and now Superintendent of Polymers Division at Tennessee Eastman, for his hard work in the early stages of TPM. He was instrumental in convincing senior management to "buy in" to the concept, and he has continually supported TPM implementation in his division.

-- Doug Moss, Industrial Engineer at Tennessee Eastman, who, in the early stages of TPM's development, was very active in generating some of the TPM process information and in developing the TPM teams.

-- Don Davis, who was one of the original pilot Primary Implementation Team Leaders in Organic Chemicals Division and who has spent many years as a TPM Coordinator on the TPM Staff at Tennessee Eastman. His production experience has contributed much to the TPM program.

-- Clyde DeVault, a TPM Coordinator at Tennessee Eastman. Clyde's craft background, apprentice training background, and experience have allowed him to make many contributions to TPM from the craft perspective.

-- Jim Carmack, who was one of the original pilot Primary Implementation Team Leaders in the Power and Services Division. Over a period of six years, Jim has helped institutionalize TPM as a "Way of Life" in his operating area.

-- W. R. Garwood, President of Tennessee Eastman, who has been very supportive in committing the necessary resources for the deployment and maintenance of the TPM process and in providing frequent reinforcement to our employees.

-- my family: my wife, Linda; my two daughters, Teresa and Trish; and my son, Neal. They all supported me in countless ways during the development of TPM.

-- Cynthia Johnson, who helped assemble, organize and edit the material in this book

List of Illustrations

1   Introduction

TPM (**Total Productive Maintenance**) is a new work system that addresses the interface problems between a company's *maintenance organization* and its *production organization.* Most American industries today are organized with maintenance on one side and operations on the other. Although both sides have the same goal -- to be a productive unit in a company making a profit -- the organizational line frequently gets in the way, causing delays and production stoppages. TPM provides a mechanism for both sides to work together as a team to improve product quality, equipment availability, and equipment reliability.

TPM (**Total Productive *Maintenance***) is the initial phase of an overall strategy called **Total Productive Management**. (See Chapter 2, "What is TPM?".)

♦ **Total Productive Management** involves skill transfer at many different levels in an organization.
♦ **Total Productive *Maintenance*** (the subject of this book) deals specifically with the operations/maintenance relationship.

TPM (**Total Productive *Maintenance***) combines operators and mechanics into a single team which identifies existing tasks that cause delays, create waste, and reduce productivity. The organizational line which normally separates the maintenance and operating functions is replaced by a "shared task zone" in which both parties are trained and certified to safely perform tasks identified by the team (See Figure 1-1 and Figure 1-2.)

The end result is that, on as as-needed basis, operators perform some tasks that were once thought to be "maintenance" tasks, and maintenance personnel perform some tasks that were once thought to be "operations" tasks. Whenever a task in the "shared task zone" needs to be performed, the individual who spots the problem can promptly take corrective action without going through two or more layers of supervision to get the message to the maintenance or operations person who is designated to do the work.

Two further outcomes of TPM are that operators assume more ownership of the equipment and mechanics become more process oriented. When these attitudes are evident, the focus of TPM then changes to using the team to eliminate unnecessary tasks and improve the equipment.

Figure 1-1 illustrates the inadequacy of the old work system. Operators and mechanics each have clearly identified skills, and both do only those skills designated as their own. If an operator observes that a pump's packing needs to be adjusted, he or she reports the problem to his or her supervisor, who initiates a work

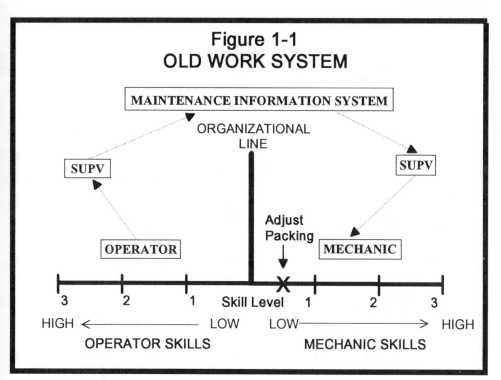

Figure 1-1
OLD WORK SYSTEM

request. The work request is transferred through the Maintenance Information System (either electronically or on paper) to the Maintenance supervisor, who will contact the mechanic and assign the job. When the mechanic arrives at the job site, he or she must find the operator and get him or her to come to the job site to shut down the pump. At this point, the work can actually be done. The organizational line has required a tremendous communications effort for the completion of a simple maintenance task. This administrative system consumes much time, promotes inefficiency, causes longer downtimes, increases costs, and decreases productivity.

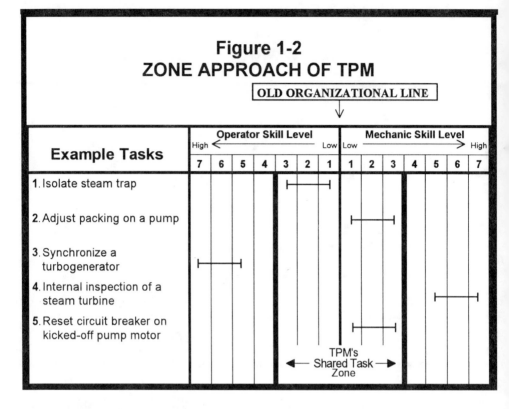

Figure 1-2 illustrates the effectiveness of TPM's zone approach. Here, operators and mechanics have formed a team to identify tasks that could be performed by either group when proper training has been given. The old organizational line, which separated the maintenance and operating functions, has been replaced by a "shared task zone" in which both operators and mechanics are trained and certified to safely perform tasks identified by the team (based on task analysis and cost benefit analysis). Since adjusting the packing is in the shared task zone, the operator who observes the need for adjusting the packing can simply do it, without the "administrative hassle" of prolonged communications with Maintenance and Operations supervisors.

Because TPM produces a radical culture change in most organizations, it is essential that it be introduced and implemented with a plan which takes into consideration its effect on all employees.

Most people don't resist change; they resist <u>being</u> changed!

Because most people resist being changed by their management, this book proposes a TPM implementation plan which allows the people who will be affected by TPM to be a part of the changes brought about by TPM. This TPM implementation plan encourages participation at every level in the organization. All people affected by TPM are given an opportunity to be a part of the process; TPM is not intended to be a program which management initiates over the objections of everyone else.

Each organization is different, and TPM implementation will reflect those differences. While the overall implementation plan is the same for all organizations, there is room for flexibility and customization of the process for your company, whatever the culture. Also, you will probably find that TPM implementation will differ from place to place in the same organization.

TPM has been successfully implemented by over 120 teams at Tennessee Eastman Division (TED) of Eastman Chemical Company in Kingsport, Tennessee. At TED, TPM is a partnership between the maintenance and production organizations which improves product quality, reduces waste, reduces manufacturing costs, increases equipment availability, and improves TED's state of maintenance. This partnership emphasizes the involvement of *all* employees in maintaining facilities and equipment. Throughout this book, case histories of actual TPM implementations at TED and at other locations will be given to illustrate various aspects of the TPM process.

Chapter 2 highlights the role of **Total Productive Maintenance** in the overall strategy of **Total Productive Management**. Also included in Chapter 2 are an explanation of interface management and a list of the basic goals and concepts of TPM. Chapter 3 focuses on the benefits of TPM, and Chapter 4 details the team structure for management and deployment of TPM. Chapters 5-7 contain the actual implementation plan, step by step. Chapter 8 emphasizes the concepts of Performance Management and their use in reinforcing employees who are participating in TPM, and Chapter 9 reviews the history of the TPM program at Tennessee Eastman Division in Kingsport, Tennessee. The book concludes with a Glossary and an Index.

2   What Is TPM?

Sections In This Chapter

I. **Total Productive Maintenance (TPM) - A Part of Total Productive Management**
II. **Interface Management: Before and After TPM**
III. **Total Productive Maintenance -- Definition**
IV. **Total Productive Maintenance -- Goals**
V. **Total Productive Maintenance -- Concepts**
VI. **Total Productive Maintenance -- Benefits**
VII. **What TPM Is *NOT***

I. Total Productive Maintenance (TPM) -- A Part of Total Productive Management

The acronym **TPM** represents several different phrases, all referring to work systems which deal with a conscientious, systematic, data-based approach to skill transfer. *Skill transfer* is the process of moving lower-level skills (tasks) from the exclusive domain of one work group to a "shared-task zone." This allows any person who has been properly trained and certified to perform a particular task to go on and perform the task, thus eliminating the delay which occurs if a different person must be contacted to do the work. (See Figure 2-1 for an example TPM task transfer chart.) The skills which are identified and placed in the "shared-task zone" by the people who do the work (*not* by management) become the responsibility of anyone who has been trained and certified to perform those skills.

Skill transfer has to do with *interface management.* The *interface* is the point of contact between two people or two groups of people who must work together to accomplish a task. See Figure 2-2.

Figure 2-2, Total Productive Management

Total Productive Management is the overall interface management strategy. It refers to skill transfer at all levels of an organization and among many different relationships which exist within an organization. Skill transfer can take place between any two people or groups of people who work together to accomplish specific tasks in serving their customers.

Total Productive Maintenance (the subject of this book) is represented in Figure 2-2 by TPM[1]. This first phase of **Total Productive Management** specifically addresses the maintenance/operations relationship. The production delays which are caused by this relationship as it exists in

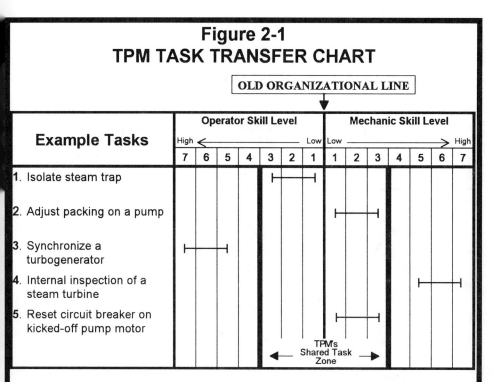

Figure 2-1
TPM TASK TRANSFER CHART

For the TPM Task Transfer Chart above, five tasks which required work requests between Operations and Maintenance were identified by the TPM Primary Implementation Team. After analysis by this team, three tasks (numbers 1, 2, and 5) were approved for the Shared Task Zone. Two tasks (numbers 3 and 4) involved high skill levels and were not suitable for transfer.

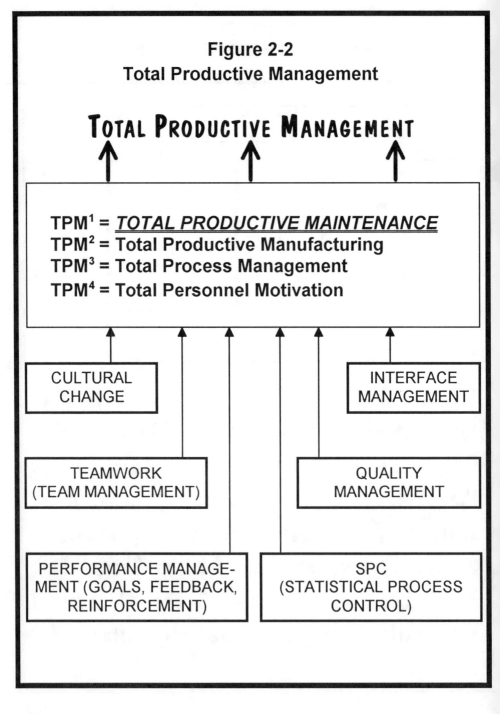

Figure 2-2
Total Productive Management

TOTAL PRODUCTIVE MANAGEMENT

TPM^1 = _**TOTAL PRODUCTIVE MAINTENANCE**_
TPM^2 = **Total Productive Manufacturing**
TPM^3 = **Total Process Management**
TPM^4 = **Total Personnel Motivation**

CULTURAL
CHANGE

INTERFACE
MANAGEMENT

TEAMWORK
(TEAM MANAGEMENT)

QUALITY
MANAGEMENT

PERFORMANCE MANAGE-
MENT (GOALS, FEEDBACK,
REINFORCEMENT)

SPC
(STATISTICAL PROCESS
CONTROL)

most companies today make implementation of TPM[1] the logical starting place for a company hoping to improve its equipment availability and reliability. In most companies, the biggest opportunities for improvement in cost reduction and equipment uptime exist at the interface of maintenance and operations. The subject of this book is TPM[1], **Total Productive Maintenance**. In all chapters of this book, the acronym **TPM** refers to TPM[1], **Total Productive Maintenance**.

Total Productive Manufacturing, represented by TPM[2], creates a partnership among all employees who have a functional part in producing the product. This next phase of **Total Productive Management** goes beyond TPM[1] and is concerned with interface management in the entire manufacturing unit. Opportunities exist for skill transfer between operators and other operators; operators and lab personnel; and lab personnel and engineers. Opportunities may also exist among other interfaces which are part of a particular manufacturing unit.

Total Process Management, represented by TPM[3], is the management of the interfaces in the total process of a line of business. Using the same tools and skills developed in TPM[1] and TPM[2], TPM[3] evolves into including the production personnel, management, engineering, supply and distribution, maintenance, service groups, and others.

Total Personnel Motivation, represented by TPM[4], is the ultimate way to manage. It can come about only by developing all employees so that they have the knowledge, skills, tools, and desire to influence the overall profitability of the process. All employees are managers of their own jobs and are empowered to improve any interface which is part of the job. The management tools which impact the **Total Productive Management** process, as shown in Figure 2-2, are essential parts of making TPM[4] effective. One of the most important tools is a reinforcement program that will create an atmosphere for continual improvement and the use of discretionary effort. TPM[4] should provide a means for all employees to expand their skills to the maximum and an incentive to do so.

Properly implemented, the four phases of **Total Productive Management** will lead a business to the ultimate point in profits and employee satisfaction.

II. Interface Management: Before and After TPM

Figure 2-3 is a representation of interface management in most organizations today. The Operator, who is the main person responsible for producing the product, depends on several other groups to accomplish this task. He interacts with General Mechanics, Electrical and Instrument Mechanics, and various other Operating Support personnel. Each time he needs services from one of these support people, he must go through his

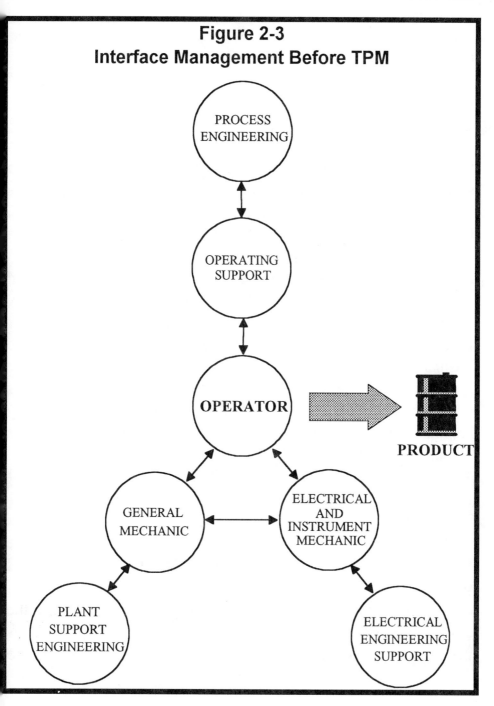

Figure 2-3
Interface Management Before TPM

management and their management to request their services. Then, he must wait until they can schedule his job and come to the job site to perform it.

The Operating Support people, in turn, may request services from Process Engineering groups. If the Operator needs a service which will ultimately be provided by Process Engineering, the delay between the request for the service and the delivery of it will be even longer.

Similarly, in order to meet the Operator's needs, the General Mechanics and the Electrical and Instrument Mechanics may need to request services from Plant Support Engineering or Electrical Engineering Support personnel. Also, one type mechanic may need to request the services of another type mechanic, demonstrating the "that's not my job" syndrome. This whole interface system, with each person or group being solely responsible for specific tasks, causes many delays and much equipment downtime.

Figure 2-4 is a representation of interface management *after* TPM has been implemented. The Operator now shares skills with the Mechanics and the Operations Support personnel. The Mechanics have analyzed their interfaces with other crafts and with the Engineering Support groups, and more skill-sharing is taking place at those interfaces. (The gray areas where the circles overlap represent the shared-skills areas.) Everyone has been raised to a higher skill level (the circles are bigger), but no

Figure 2-4
Interface Management After TPM

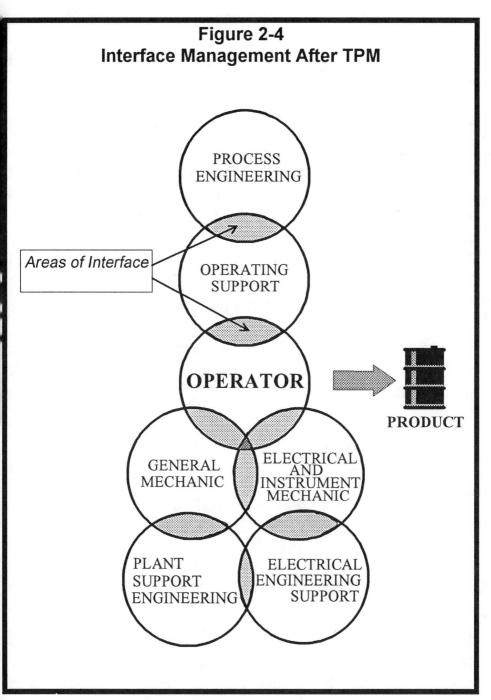

additional personnel have been hired. Productivity is up, and equipment downtime is reduced.

Many delays in waiting for service have been eliminated because each person now has been trained and certified to perform tasks which fall into the areas where the circles overlap. Tasks that previously required the Operator to contact one other person to get a job done (for example, the General Mechanic) are now accomplished in one-fourth the time. Tasks that previously required two contacts (for example, Operator to General Mechanic, then General Mechanic to Plant Support Engineer) are accomplished in one-ninth the time.

With skill transfer occurring in the entire organization, product quality is improved, waste and costs are reduced, and the overall state of maintenance is improved.

III. Total Productive Maintenance -- Definition

> *Total Productive Maintenance is a conscientious, systematic, data-based approach to skill transfer.*

Total Productive Maintenance is a new work system that addresses the interface problems between the maintenance organization and the production organization. Based on a partnership between operations and maintenance, TPM helps operators and mechanics to become multi-skilled. Teams composed primarily of operators and maintenance personnel (*not* management) identify and analyze the tasks for transfer, develop and perform the training, implement the task transfer, and monitor the success of the program. TPM is driven by decisions from the bottom up -- not by management mandate. It focuses on people, productivity, and improvements to achieve enhanced earnings for the company.

IV. Total Productive Maintenance -- Goals

The major goals of TPM are to:

- Improve product quality
- Reduce waste
- Improve the state of maintenance
- Empower employees

The implementation of TPM will produce many other benefits, such as job enrichment, safety enhancement, and improved flexibility of workers. However, most organizations find it difficult to focus on many different things at once. Therefore, the four goals listed above are the usual focus of TPM implementation.

V. Total Productive Maintenance -- Concepts

TPM's goals are accomplished through one or more of the following concepts:

1. Operators doing routine maintenance
2. Operators assisting mechanics when equipment is down
3. Mechanics assisting operators with shutdowns/start-ups
4. Transfer of tasks not requiring craftworkers
5. Team approach to computerized calibration
6. Transfer of tasks between operating groups
7. Multi-skilling of craftworkers

The idea behind these concepts, which were developed at Tennessee Eastman Division, is that operators and mechanics can work together to understand how their roles interact and what they must do to support one another in providing equipment maintenance. The following paragraphs further explain each concept.

1. **Empowering operators to perform specified routine maintenance tasks on their equipment**

   Operators assuming ownership of their equipment helps to eliminate potential causes of failure. By taking care of dust, rattles, loosened bolts, scratches, deformation, and wear, all of which combine to cause failures, the operators can do their part to prevent failures. Operators may also perform repair tasks to restore equipment to operating status.

The operators are properly trained and certified to perform the specifically identified tasks. Also, the proper tools and supplies required to perform the tasks are provided. Operators are given the training and tools to perform the "CLAIR" tasks -- Clean, Lube, Adjust, Inspect, and Repair.

> ### CLAIR Tasks
>
> C = Clean
> L = Lubricate
> A = Adjust
> I = Inspect
> R = Repair

Safety is given utmost consideration in training individuals to perform tasks identified by the TPM teams.

2. Empowering operators to assist mechanics in the repair of equipment when it is down

Frequently, several pieces of equipment fail at the same time, and there are not enough maintenance personnel to respond promptly. In such cases, the operators may be sent home because equipment is down for an extended period. Under this concept, operators are trained to assist maintenance personnel in the repair of equipment. The maintenance force is enlarged; the operators do not lose pay due to lack of work; and ultimately, the failed equipment is returned to service more quickly.

3. **Empowering mechanics to assist operators in the shutdown and start-up of equipment**

There are times when operators need assistance in shutting down and/or starting up equipment but do not have the help. This prolongs the shutdown and causes maintenance personnel to wait. By using properly trained mechanics to help operators get the equipment shut down, the downtime of the equipment is reduced.

Once the mechanics finish the repairs, they assist the operators in returning the equipment to service by correcting leaks and other mechanical or electrical problems as they occur. By staying at the job site and assisting until the operators have the equipment running, the mechanics eliminated many repeat calls, and overall downtime is reduced.

Also, mechanics can be trained to perform some of the operations tasks without the assistance of operators.

4. **Empowering lower-skilled personnel to perform routine jobs not requiring skilled craftworkers**

There are many routine tasks at TED that can be done by just about anyone who has been given proper tools and training. Under the TPM program, these tasks are identified. If it is not feasible for skilled operators or mechanics to do the job, lower bracket people are used. As the maintenance personnel spend less time on routine work and emergency response work, they can concentrate more on improving equipment reliability and doing the work for which they have been specially trained.

5. **Use of computerized technology to enable operators to calibrate selected instruments**

Quality Management at TED requires that instruments be properly calibrated. The use of Statistical Process Control (SPC) charts to control operations is based on process feedback that is as accurate as possible. As part of the TPM program, instrument calibration test units were purchased. These units enable more effective SPC by allowing people to routinely check and monitor the calibration of critical instruments.

6. Transfer of tasks between operating groups

Through natural evolution, operating job structures frequently develop which are not as practical as desired. In many cases, unnecessary wait times and equipment downtime are the attendant results. Identifying these nonproductive interfaces and restructuring job responsibilities can remove such inefficiencies.

7. Multi-skilling of craftworkers

The focus of this concept is training mechanics, electricians, and other craftworkers to use the zone approach in analyzing their job interfaces. Frequently, if an electrician learns some mechanical skills and a mechanic learns some electrical skills, further reductions can be made in equipment downtime.

Multi-skilling also reduces the number of times an operator hears, "It's not a mechanical problem; you need to get an electrician," or, "It's not an electrical problem; you need to get a mechanic." Multi-skilled craftworkers become stewards of the problem and lose the "that's not my job" attitude.

VI. Total Productive Maintenance - Benefits

- Improved Product Quality

Case History 2-A

At TED, during the start-up of a polymer production line, we were able to qualify the polymer as Class I product in less time because of TPM. The off-class product generated during start-up dropped from 90,000 pounds/year to 19,000 pounds/year. Over a year's time, this is worth approximately $2,000,000 in Class I polymer production.

- Reduced Cost

Case History 2-B

In TED's Air Conditioning Services group, the operators have documented $ 3.5 million in 'TPM' savings in maintenance and operations time from 1987 through 1991. The operators now change their own thermostats, drive belts, control valves, tubing, and so on.

- Improved Equipment Reliability and Uptime

Case History 2-C

In TED's Organic Chemicals Division, the norm for rupture disc replacements was 17 per month. Since implementation of TPM, operators are more sensitive to the importance of carefully charging and emptying the reactors to prevent damage to the rupture discs. With this type of operator ownership, rupture disc failures have been significantly reduced to about 1 per month.

- Job Enrichment

Case History 2-D

TPM creates an environment in which operators feel better about operating their equipment. They like doing minor repairs. For example, changing idler gears was a task that was transferred from mechanics to operators in TED's Fibers Division. The number of idler gear failures has gone from over 50 per week to less than 8 per week. With more responsibility and ownership, people can better achieve continual improvement.

- Promotion of Teamwork Between Operations and Maintenance

Case History 2-E

Before TPM, when a pump needed to be replaced, two mechanics were sent to do the job while the operator waited. Now, only one mechanic is sent, and the operator assists in repairing and/or replacing the pump. Delay time is reduced and productivity is increased.

Case History 2-F

On December 26, 1989, TED experienced a major power failure which shut down the entire plant. If TED had been without TPM, approximately 1200 craftworkers would have been the primary workforce to execute plant repairs. However, because of TPM (the operators trained on maintenance skills), there were several thousand operators assisting the craftworkers. Because of TPM, the plant was started up three days sooner than would have been possible otherwise.

- Improved Skills/Flexibility (Operator and Mechanic)

Case History 2-G

Under TPM, operators and mechanics were trained/certified to de-energize, re-energize, and reset electrical equipment. Over a five-year period, the number of requests for electrical specialists to perform these tasks dropped 44% (from over 29,000 requests to around 17,000). This TPM-acquired skill has improved the flexibility of all non-electrical employees.

- Higher Quality Maintenance Service

Case History 2-H

In one situation, a mechanic was asked, "How has TPM helped you?" He replied, "Now, I can do a quality repair and find the root cause of the failure. Before TPM, I used to have to hurry up and just fix the breakdown."

- Safety Enhancement

> ## Case History 2-I
>
> Under TPM, operators and mechanics have been taught the proper way to do the tasks. TPM has enhanced safety because the TPM process focuses on safety. In over five years, performing approximately one million TPM tasks, TPM-trained personnel have reported only four minor injuries.

- Reduction of Product Contamination

> ## Case History 2-J
>
> In TED's Fibers Division, mechanics were busy "fighting fires" and had little time to do the preventive maintenance on hydraulic oil systems. As a result, many oil leaks contaminated the products. When operators were trained to perform TPM tasks, the mechanics had more time to devote to the preventive maintenance on hydraulic leaks. The number of leaks dropped from approximately 20 per week to less than 10 per week.

VII. What TPM Is *NOT*

- TPM is *not* a maintenance program.

- TPM is *not* another method to reduce costs.

- TPM is *not* a ploy to take care of reductions in personnel.

- TPM is *not* a way to eliminate craftworkers (electricians, mechanics, instrument experts, and others).

- TPM is *not* a silver bullet that solves all the problems.

- TPM is *not* making craftworkers out of operators.

3   Why Use TPM?

```
Sections In This Chapter

  I.   Current Influences on Today's Companies
 II.   Who Can Use TPM?
III.   Why Should Your Company Use TPM?
```

I. Current Influences on Today's Companies

Total Productive Maintenance provides a way for companies to deal with many of the influences which face them today.

► Because of today's *global competition*, companies cannot continue to operate in the same old, inefficient ways. Benchmarking against the best in the world forces changes in "the way we've always done it."

► The *changing culture* in the work force is evidenced by the proliferation of management strategies involving people empowerment and team management. More and more workers want and expect to be involved in teamwork situations rather than traditional line management systems.

► The *competitive advantage* sought by most companies is improved by TPM. In order to enhance the state of maintenance, maintenance must be managed in a way different from our traditional systems.

► *Continual improvement* is as necessary in management technology as it is in manufacturing technology. Up to now, management technology has lagged behind, using old management methods for new technologies and new work philosophies. TPM provides a transition for management from the old to the new.

II. Who Can Use TPM?

► Companies with Multiple Job Descriptions
► Companies Seeking Enhanced Earnings
► Companies with Multiple Cultures

III. Why Should Your Company Use TPM?

♦ TPM will save your company money.

The savings will come primarily from elimination of delays and work stoppages. It has been estimated that breakdown maintenance costs 10 times more and takes 4 times longer than planned maintenance. If operators are trained to prevent failures, the savings are great.

◆ TPM will improve product quality.

Product quality is improved because the operators, by responding quickly to an interruption in a process, can prevent subsequent adjustment of the reactants and possible production of off-class material. See Case History 3-A.

Case History 3-A

At TED, in a time-dependent batch process taking place in a pressure vessel stirred by an electric agitator, non-electrical problems (high viscosity or a chunk of material in the reactants) would cause an occasional interruption in the power supply to the agitator, causing it to quit stirring. When the stirring would cease, the reactants would begin to crystallize.

Before TPM, the operator was required to call a control system mechanic. Depending on the priority of the area, the mechanic would be there within one to two hours of the need. Meanwhile, the reaction would still be taking place and crystallizing, possibly clogging the whole piece of machinery.

Under TPM, the operator can often respond immediately to the stopped agitator by going into the electric control room and resetting the circuit breaker. The agitator begins to stir the reactants again, and the operator has prevented the loss of the entire batch and/or the production of off-class material.

- TPM will enhance safety.

Without TPM, often operators and mechanics may take unsafe short cuts to simplify their jobs. They may not have the proper tools, training, or supplies to safely do a job. One example is an operator using adjustable pliers instead of the appropriate box end wrench. TPM provides the proper training, tools, supplies and authorization, thus enhancing safety.

- TPM will reduce waste.

TPM's goals include using equipment to its maximum effectiveness and elimination of waste and losses caused by equipment. See Case History 3-B.

Case History 3-B

In many continuous processes, the product continues to flow when minor interruptions occur. Before TPM, the product flow would be directed to a waste receptacle while the operator was waiting for the mechanic to come. Under TPM, with operators able to handle minor problems as they arise, as much as 75% reduction in waste can be realized during an outage.

◆ TPM will improve the state of your maintenance.

As mentioned earlier, reactive maintenance (responding to breakdown failures) is more expensive than planned maintenance. Under TPM, the operators (1) become "owners" of their equipment, (2) are more aware of what the equipment is supposed to do, and (3) are capable of doing minor repairs, adjustment checks and preventive maintenance. In these conditions, maintenance personnel and craftworkers are freed to concentrate on quality repairs and equipment improvement, instead of spending their time "fighting fires."

◆ TPM will improve the equipment availability (uptime) in your plant.

Less time will be spent waiting for maintenance personnel. Our interface management studies at TED have shown that it takes four times longer to return a piece of equipment to service if the person who discovers the problem must call another person to repair the equipment rather than doing the repair when the problem is found. If operators, mechanics, and electrical-and- instrument personnel are empowered to do low-skill tasks themselves, without calling for additional help, they can put the equipment back in production as much as 75% faster.

• TPM will improve teamwork between operators and mechanics.

Prior to TPM at TED, mechanics met in their own natural unit teams, operators met in *their* own natural unit teams, and they had very little direct communication with each other. Most communication took place by going though the proper levels of management. (See Figure 1-1 in Chapter 1, *Introduction.*)   Operators were trained to operate the equipment; maintenance people were trained to fix the equipment. With TPM, they work together to discover areas in which they can empower each other. When they start sharing knowledge and skills, they not only talk about the job, but they also talk about their families and hobbies, producing more feelings of friendship. Teamwork efforts are improved because the craftworker/operator barrier has been broken down. They are now working as a team to produce the product.

• TPM will provide job enrichment and improve operator responsibility.

A group of operators was surveyed to discover *why* they liked TPM. Their answers were:

1. We have more control over our jobs.
2. We see immediate results. "I fixed it."
3. We have pride in the results.
4. We like the recognition for doing the tasks.

5. Preventing the problems makes our jobs easier.
6. We feel the company "trusts" us by giving us tools.
7. We enjoy being part of making equipment improvements.

◆ TPM will cause a reduction in emergency work. See Case History 3-C.

Case History 3-C

In TED's Organic Chemicals Division, craftworkers were not scheduled to work during non-normal working hours. (Normal working hours are 8:00 a.m. to 5:00 p.m., Monday - Friday.) Before TPM, this division would generate 250 off-hour emergency calls in a year for craftworkers. After TPM, the number fell to 75 calls a year. At the same time, production increased 80%. This tremendous reduction in emergency calls to the maintenance organization happened because the operators were empowered to deal with emergencies themselves.

---

* TPM will cause a reduction in the time that maintenance personnel spend on low-skill jobs, allowing them to spend more time improving the equipment.

From TED's TPM data, we estimate that 15% of a maintenance organization's current responsibilities can be absorbed by existing operators. Even more maintenance tasks can be shared with operations if the number of operators is increased.

* TPM will improve the skills and flexibility of all employees.

For a diagram representing this benefit, see Figure 2-4 in Chapter 2, *What Is TPM?*. By sharing skills and cross-training each other, all the operators, mechanics, and support personnel have increased their skill levels. Each one is better equipped to respond to the needs of the equipment. Individual productivity is up, and equipment downtime is reduced.

* TPM is compatible with many of the current management strategies used in American plants today (Statistical Process Control (SPC), team management, performance management, high-performance teams). TPM will enhance these management strategies.

4

Team Structure of TPM

> ## Sections In This Chapter
>
> **I.** Introduction to Teams
> **II.** TPM, Team Management, and Accountability
> **III.** TPM Teams
> **IV.** Responsibilities of Key TPM Positions

I. Introduction to Teams

The plan recommended in this book for implementation of TPM relies heavily on the concept of teamwork. By "teamwork," or "team management," we mean the management system that organizes people into *natural unit teams* and/or *high performance teams* in order to accomplish a company's stated goals and objectives. At TED, teams are charged with contributing to continual improvement of customer satisfaction and business success by achieving team goals through empowerment, regular meetings, and cooperative, systematic efforts. At TED, each team meets approximately one hour each week. Each meeting has a predetermined agenda, and a large portion of the meeting time is spent on problem-solving.

A *natural unit team* is one which is formed around the existing organizational structure. Teams are expected to work on problems within their control, but they often find that many of the problems they are trying to solve cut across team boundaries. Many times, the natural unit team structure does not facilitate the right ownership of the problems and does not get the right people involved in solving those problems.

A *high performance team* brings together people from two or more different natural unit organizations to produce an empowered group that is better able to manage and solve those problems that affect more than one natural unit team. TPM teams are high performance, interfacing teams made up of people from different organizations that have a common interest. Many "supervisors" are thus called "team managers" as the teams become more self-directing.

An effective team:

- Achieves business results.
- Has documented goals and supporting plans.
- Exhibits responsibility for clearly defined processes.
- Is accountable to itself and higher level teams.
- Assesses its progress.
- Has good documentation.
- Has everyone's participation.
- Uses quality improvement tools.
- Has a skilled leader and members.

Team management is based on the principle of interlocking teams, up and down the organization. Figure 4-1, Interlocking Natural Unit Teams, is a representation of interlocking teams in Operations and Maintenance. Usually, interlocking teams are natural unit teams. The most basic natural unit team on the Operations side is composed of one crew's members and their leader (supervisor). (See triangle 1.) The four crews that are necessary to handle all shifts are four natural unit teams. The next natural unit team, one level up, would be the crew supervisors and the second level manager to whom they report. (See triangle 2.) The next natural unit Operations team has the second level managers (senior engineers) for members and the department head for a team leader. (See triangle 3.) Except for the crew members in triangle 1, every person is on two teams--on one team as a leader and on the other team as a member. This structure extends up the production organization to the company president.

The Maintenance function is organized in a similar manner, with crew-level teams in triangle 5 reporting on up through higher teams to the company president in triangle 9.

All natural unit teams contribute to the achievement of company goals. However, without TPM, the Operations teams usually focus on production; Maintenance teams usually focus on maintenance. TPM builds a partnership, generating teams made up of members of both Operations and Maintenance natural unit teams. TPM allows interface management among natural unit teams and team management across the organization. TPM

Figure 4-1
Interlocking Natural Unit Teams

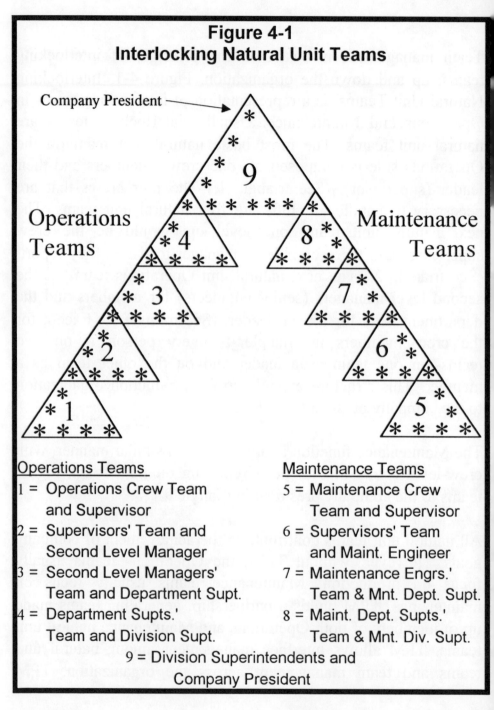

Company President

Operations
Teams

Maintenance
Teams

Operations Teams
1 = Operations Crew Team
   and Supervisor
2 = Supervisors' Team and
   Second Level Manager
3 = Second Level Managers'
   Team and Department Supt.
4 = Department Supts.'
   Team and Division Supt.

Maintenance Teams
5 = Maintenance Crew
   Team and Supervisor
6 = Supervisors' Team
   and Maint. Engineer
7 = Maintenance Engrs.'
   Team & Mnt. Dept. Supt.
8 = Maint. Dept. Supts.'
   Team & Mnt. Div. Supt.

9 = Division Superintendents and
Company President

teams are special teams set up just to administrate TPM; the team members have common interests and work in the same community. Once TPM is well established, the TPM teams can be disbanded. Then, the main focus for both groups is on equipment reliability as it impacts production of the product.

Figure 4-2 is a representation of TPM teams functioning alongside the natural unit teams. TPM teams do not replace the natural unit teams; they allow better management of the interfaces that occur as the Operations and Maintenance natural unit teams interact to do their jobs. Normally, a TPM Coordinator meets with each TPM team.

II. TPM, Team Management, and Accountability

An important side effect of TPM is that the barriers between Maintenance and Operations are lowered. These barriers are the procedures and practices which are followed to get approval to perform certain tasks. Typical examples are going through the chain of command to take a machine out of production and filling out work orders in order to get the services of Maintenance people.

The real reason for these barriers is to ensure precise accountability. Where resources (such as a mechanic's time) are limited, we must have ways to ensure that they are effectively used. Scheduling is impossible without some logical labor distribution process. Unfortunately, sometimes the very success of these labor distribution systems prevents us from seeking

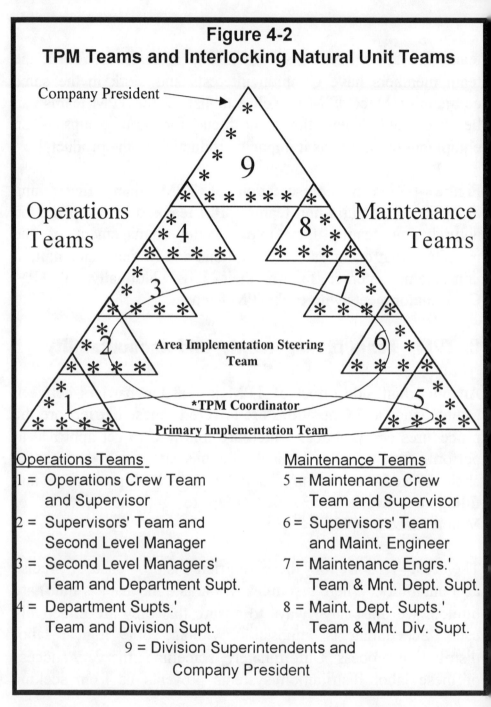

Figure 4-2
TPM Teams and Interlocking Natural Unit Teams

Company President →

9

Operations
Teams

4

8

Maintenance
Teams

3

7

2

6

Area Implementation Steering
Team

1

*TPM Coordinator

5

Primary Implementation Team

Operations Teams	Maintenance Teams
1 = Operations Crew Team and Supervisor	5 = Maintenance Crew Team and Supervisor
2 = Supervisors' Team and Second Level Manager	6 = Supervisors' Team and Maint. Engineer
3 = Second Level Managers' Team and Department Supt.	7 = Maintenance Engrs.' Team & Mnt. Dept. Supt.
4 = Department Supts.' Team and Division Supt.	8 = Maint. Dept. Supts.' Team & Mnt. Div. Supt.

9 = Division Superintendents and
Company President

better methods of achieving the same ends. In TPM, the goal is "increased machine utilization," not "increased accountability." TPM directs the organization's efforts toward increases in equipment utilization in such a way that many standard practices are questioned. Because it reassigns responsibility for some of the basic tasks required to achieve maximum output, the entire structure of accountability must be reexamined. It is for this reason that TPM relies heavily on Team Management as a basic driving force behind the process.

When the accountability structure changes, everyone is impacted. Long-standing work practices will probably be disrupted. This will increase the amount of time and care that managers must devote to their people and their people's concerns. The best way to deal with the natural resistance to change is to assure that each involved manager is directly involved with making the process work.

For this reason, all managers who are going to be directly affected by TPM should be given the opportunity to make a positive contribution to TPM's success. Teams are an excellent vehicle for making this happen. This also prevents all the work from falling on just a few shoulders and makes TPM a much less intensive management effort than it would be if other management structures were used.

Not all TPM teams are permanent. Some teams function for a short while, and then become inactive unless they are needed. Some teams may disband altogether after the program is up and running. However, some teams will remain in effect and meet on a regular basis until TPM is fully integrated as a "way of life." Some teams are needed to sustain TPM once it is fully implemented.

III. TPM Teams

The team structure for TPM implementation includes the following teams:

- TPM Staff
- Feasibility Team
- Company Policy/Steering Team
- Division Policy/Steering Team
- Area Implementation Steering Team
- Primary Implementation Team

Figure 4-3, Team Structure of TPM, shows the relationship of the above-listed teams. However, bear in mind that the team structure of TPM is directly related to the size of your organization. If your organization is large, you may need more levels of policy/steering teams. If your organization is small, then the functions of the Feasibility Team, Company Policy/Steering Team, Division Policy/Steering Team, and Area Implementation Steering Team may all be performed by the same group of people.

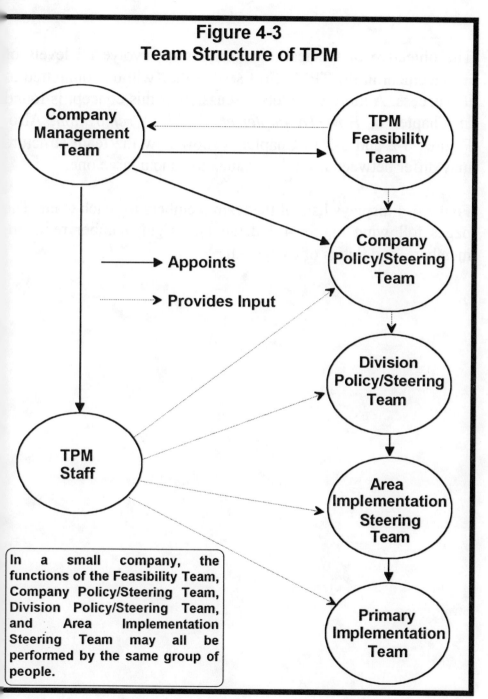

Figure 4-3
Team Structure of TPM

Company Management Team

TPM Feasibility Team

→ Appoints

┈┈┈→ Provides Input

Company Policy/Steering Team

Division Policy/Steering Team

TPM Staff

Area Implementation Steering Team

In a small company, the functions of the Feasibility Team, Company Policy/Steering Team, Division Policy/Steering Team, and Area Implementation Steering Team may all be performed by the same group of people.

Primary Implementation Team

The objective of the team structure is to involve all levels of management in the TPM effort so that they will be committed to its success. A more complete discussion of this concept is found in Chapter 6, *How To Implement TPM - Preparation*. Also, Figures 6-2 and 6-3 in Chapter 6 show how the team structure may differ between a small organization and a large one.

Figure 4-4 displays lists of the team members for each team. The pages following Figure 4-4 detail the origin, number required, members, and duties of each team.

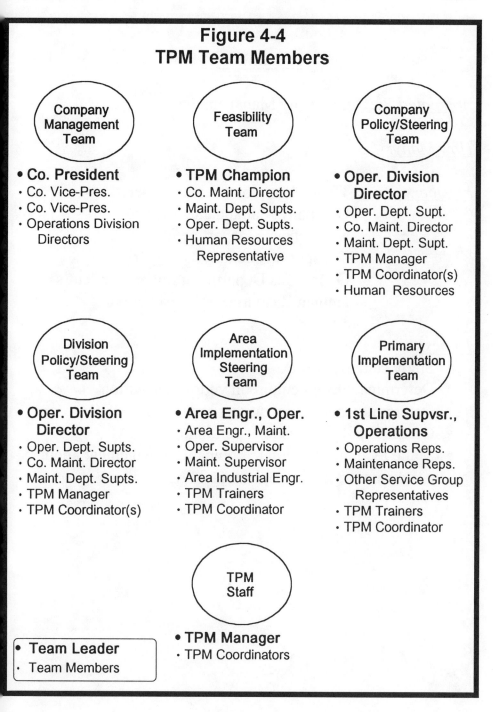

Figure 4-4
TPM Team Members

Company Management Team

- **Co. President**
  · Co. Vice-Pres.
  · Co. Vice-Pres.
  · Operations Division Directors

Feasibility Team

- **TPM Champion**
  · Co. Maint. Director
  · Maint. Dept. Supts.
  · Oper. Dept. Supts.
  · Human Resources Representative

Company Policy/Steering Team

- **Oper. Division Director**
  · Oper. Dept. Supt.
  · Co. Maint. Director
  · Maint. Dept. Supt.
  · TPM Manager
  · TPM Coordinator(s)
  · Human Resources

Division Policy/Steering Team

- **Oper. Division Director**
  · Oper. Dept. Supts.
  · Co. Maint. Director
  · Maint. Dept. Supts.
  · TPM Manager
  · TPM Coordinator(s)

Area Implementation Steering Team

- **Area Engr., Oper.**
  · Area Engr., Maint.
  · Oper. Supervisor
  · Maint. Supervisor
  · Area Industrial Engr.
  · TPM Trainers
  · TPM Coordinator

Primary Implementation Team

- **1st Line Supvsr., Operations**
  · Operations Reps.
  · Maintenance Reps.
  · Other Service Group Representatives
  · TPM Trainers
  · TPM Coordinator

TPM Staff

- **TPM Manager**
  · TPM Coordinators

- **Team Leader**
  · Team Members

Feasibility Team

Appointed By: Company Management

How Many: 1

Members: TPM Champion (Team Leader)
Company Maintenance Director
Maintenance Department
    Superintendent(s)
Operations Department Superintendent(s)
Human Resources Representative

Duties:
   ◆ Study state of the art
   ◆ Determine current culture in your organization
   ◆ Determine your organization's readiness for TPM
   ◆ Consider policy questions pertaining to TPM
   ◆ Make recommendation to company management about
       whether or not to implement TPM

TPM Staff

Appointed By: Company Management

How Many: 1

Members: TPM Manager (Team Leader)
TPM Coordinators (1 or more, depending
  on the size of your organization)

Duties:
+ Manage the company TPM effort
+ Oversee TPM implementation in each area
+ Serve on Area Implementation Steering Teams
+ Serve on Primary Implementation Teams
+ Serve on TPM Policy/Steering Team(s)

> NOTE: For a complete check list of the TPM
> Coordinator's duties, see Chapters 6 and 7. A
> "TPM Coordinator's Check List" box is provided
> with each implementation process step for which
> this person bears the major responsibility. Each
> section containing a "TPM Coordinator's Check
> List" box is designated with an arrow (➡).

Company Policy/Steering Team

Appointed By: Company Management

How Many: 1

Members: Operating Division Director (Team Leader)
Operating Department Superintendent
Company Maintenance Director
Maintenance Department Superintendent
TPM Manager
TPM Coordinator(s)
Human Resources Representative

Duties:
- Set up a TPM management structure
- Establish accountability for TPM teams
- Set measures for management involvement
- Choose TPM pilot areas
- Select personnel for key TPM assignments
- Decide TPM policy issues (pay for skills, train on overtime, tool policy, and others)
- Develop rewards/recognition plan for TPM teams
- Develop overall baseline data
- Develop pilot implementation schedule
- Develop detailed TPM deployment process

Division Policy/Steering Team

NOTE: In larger companies, this TPM team may be needed for two reasons: (1) to involve this level of management in the TPM implementation effort, and (2) to allow this level of management to determine TPM policies that may apply to its specific unit within the company. Some TPM policies may differ according to manufacturing practices and design. For example, TPM policies may differ between units with continuous processes and batch processes, or between units producing fibers and those producing chemicals.

In a small company, these functions may be performed by the same people who were on the Feasibility Team and the Company Policy Team.

Appointed By: Division Management

How Many: 1 per division

Members: Operating Division Director (Team Leader)
Operating Department Superintendents
Company Maintenance Director
Maintenance Department Superintendents
TPM Manager
TPM Coordinator(s)

Duties:
- Approve TPM implementation
- Publicize TPM endorsement
- Schedule area implementation steering team meetings and plan agendas
- Help conduct meetings
- Publish memos appointing area implementation steering team members and defining their responsibilities
- Support implementation steering teams
- Support recognition/reinforcement efforts
- Review team leader responsibilities with implementation steering team leader
- Provide response to questions/concerns
- Assist with presentations/updates to higher teams
- Assist with reinforcement planning and delivery
- Facilitate measure development
- Be a catalyst to keep it moving
- Be available
- Support TPM as a "Way of Life"

<u>Area Implementation Steering Team</u>

Appointed By: Division Policy/Steering Team (or
                  Company Policy/Steering Team)

How Many: 1 per implementation area

Members: Area Engineer, Operations (Team Leader)
                  Area Engineer, Maintenance
                  Operations Supervisor
                  Maintenance Supervisor
                  Area Industrial Engineer
                  TPM Trainers (Ad hoc members)
                  TPM Coordinator

Duties:
  - Identify implementation area
  - Appoint implementation team
  - Appoint implementation team leader
  - Recommend TPM trainers (Maintenance and Operations)
  - Recommend implementation plans to Division
    Policy/Steering Team
  - Clarify objectives (needs/expectations) for the Primary
    Implementation Teams
  - Announce TPM goals and techniques
  - Assist TPM Coordinator with crew orientation sessions
  - Provide implementation antecedents
    - Kickoff meeting
    - Support team meetings

53

- Assign resources
+ Determine reinforcement and delivery plan
  - Develop reinforcement milestones
+ Review/Approve task recommendations
+ Provide reinforcement/feedback to Primary Implementation Team
+ Provide resources for task training and equipment improvements
+ Provide periodic progress reports to Division Steering Team
+ Track TPM results
+ Ensure that TPM is reinforcing to the employees
+ Use Performance Management to manage supervisors and Primary Implementation Team members
+ Define/Develop measures for monitoring results of TPM
  - Determine plan for collecting, analyzing, and distributing measure data
  - Develop forms for data collection
  - Develop system for data analysis and report generation (computerized approach recommended)
  - Assign person to perform data analysis and generate reports
+ Develop system for maintaining history of TPM training tasks
+ Review/Approve equipment improvement opportunities
+ Identify other areas for TPM pilots
+ Develop plans for long term support of TPM
+ Support TPM as a "Way of Life"

Primary Implementation Team

Appointed By: Area Implementation Steering Team

How Many: 1 per implementation area

Members: First Line Supervisor, Operations (Team
                   Leader)
               Operations Representatives
               Maintenance Representatives
               Other Service Group Representatives
               TPM Trainers
               TPM Coordinator

Duties:
- Identify potential TPM tasks (See Figure 2-1 in Chapter 2, *What Is TPM?*.)
- Select TPM tasks
- Complete task analysis
  - Task Analysis Worksheet (Figure 7-1)
  - Time Savings Worksheets (Figures 7-2 and 7-3)
- Recommend task sharing plans to Area Implementation Steering Team
- Provide feedback to crews
- Support implementation in area
- Identify equipment improvements

IV. Responsibilities of Key TPM Positions

The following pages list the major responsibilities for some of the key people in the TPM implementation process.

<u>Primary Implementation Team Leader</u>

Appointed By: Area Implementation Steering Team

Responsibilities:
- Plan agenda for meetings
- Conduct meetings - report on results and status
- Schedule meetings
- See that meeting notes are taken and distributed
- Make sure team understands goals and objectives
- Keep Implementation Steering Team and Primary Implementation Team notified of progress, concerns, and recommendations
- Keep TPM concepts and benefits before the team
- Encourage team participation and involvement
- Arrange for support and consultations with others
- Present TPM concepts to everyone involved with the implementation
- Work with the Area Implementation Steering Team and TPM staff to:
  - develop/deliver training
  - procure tools/supplies
- Assist in establishing TPM measures and feedback systems

Area Implementation Steering Team Leader

Appointed By: Division Policy/Steering Team

Responsibilities:
- Plan agenda for meetings
- Conduct meetings - report on results and status
- Schedule meetings
- See that meeting notes are taken and distributed
- Keep Division Steering Team notified of implementation progress, concerns, and/or recommendations
- Interface support with Primary Implementation Team
- Reinforce Primary Implementation Team
- Work through the Implementation Steering Team to encourage TPM as a "way of life" concept
- Assist in establishing TPM measures and feedback system

The TPM Trainer

Appointed By: Area Implementation Steering Team

Responsibilities:
- Serve on the Implementation Steering Team and the Primary Implementation Team
- Develop/present training for TPM tasks
- Provide "on-call" support during task training cycle
- Provide encouragement/retraining as appropriate
- Certify operator/mechanic proficiency on TPM tasks

Maintenance First-Line Supervisor

Responsibilities:

- Develop working knowledge of TPM concepts and program
- Take a proactive position in implementing TPM in the area served
- Be actively involved in educating Maintenance employees in TPM concepts
- Be actively involved with Operations counterpart to identify TPM opportunities
- Be actively involved as TPM team member
- Support development/use of TPM measures
- Provide Maintenance resources to support TPM implementation
- Work with Operations to develop plans for improving equipment availability
- Track TPM implementation progress in the area served
- Provide TPM progress reports to department/division management
- Work with TPM staff to improve TPM program
- Actively pursue TPM as a "Way of Life" for improving Maintenance support in client areas

Area Industrial Engineer

Responsibilities:
- Serve on Area Implementation Steering Team
- Assist with the identification and refinement of measures
- Assist with the collection and interpretation of data
- Support Area Implementation Steering Team and the Primary Implementation Team in presenting recommendations

TPM Coordinator

Responsibilities:
- Keep abreast of TPM technology developments
- Actively pursue improvements to TPM concepts and implementation process
- Provide implementation support to Area Implementation Steering Teams and Primary Implementation Teams
- Provide administrative assistance to team leaders
- Support trainers in developing/delivering training
- Encourage and support both recognition and reinforcement to support TPM implementation
- Provide continuing implementation support to encourage TPM as a "Way of Life"

The above list of responsibilities describes only the general responsibilities of the TPM Coordinator. A TPM Coordinator meets with each Area Implementation Steering Team and Primary Implementation Team every time they meet and performs many specific duties in working with the TPM teams. Chapter 6, *How to Implement TPM - Preparation*, and Chapter 7, *How to Implement TPM - Deployment*, are written with the TPM Coordinator in mind and contain detailed task lists for this position.

5 How To Implement TPM - Overview

The following outline should be used to implement TPM. TPM's two phases, Preparation and Deployment, are fully explained in Chapters 6 and 7. This chapter contains a brief outline for each phase.

> NOTE: After the appointment of the TPM Staff and the TPM Coordinators, the implementation process is managed by the TPM Coordinator. The TPM Coordinator is responsible for initiating the implementation process in a specific area and following it through to completion. In this chapter and in Chapters 6-7, the steps which the TPM Coordinator must oversee are designated with an arrow (➡).

Preparation (Chapter 6)

I. Sell TPM and Gain Management's Commitment
   A. "Sales Pitch" Outline
   B. Explanation of "Sales Pitch" Outline
II. Feasibility Team
   A. Appointment and Membership
   B. Responsibilities of Feasibility Team

63

1. Determine State of the Art
2. Determine Current Culture - Your Locale
3. Determine Readiness for TPM
4. Other Feasibility Considerations
   a. Outline
   b. Explanation of Outline
5. Make Recommendation to Management

III. Make Go/No Go Decision
IV. TPM Staff
    A. Appoint TPM Staff
    B. Develop TPM Implementation Plan (Figure 5-1)
V. Company Policy/Steering Team
    A. Appointment and Membership
    B. Responsibilities of Company Pol./Str. Team
       1. Set Up TPM Management Structure
       2. Establish Accountability
       3. Measure Management Involvement
       4. Choose First Implementation Division
       5. Make TPM Key Individual Assignments
       6. Decide Policy/Procedural Issues
       7. Develop Rewards/Recognition Plan
       8. Develop Overall Baseline Data (Plant Level)
       9. Develop Pilot Implementation Schedule
       10. Develop Detailed TPM Deployment Process (Figure 5-2)
➤ VI. TPM Publicity and Education
    A. TPM Information
    B. Performance Management Information

VII. Formation of Division Policy/Steering Team
VIII. Selection of Implementation Area in Division
IX. Appointment of Area Implementation Steering Team
X. Pilot Baseline Established

Deployment (Chapter 7)

I. Primary Implementation Team Appointed
II. Plan for TPM Workshop
III. TPM Workshop
IV. Summarize/Publish Workshop Results
V. Conduct Review Meeting with Area Implementation Steering Team
VI. Develop Training Procedures
VII. Arrange for Tools and Supplies
VIII. Develop Area-Specific Training Plan
IX. Develop Measures and Plans for Monitoring
X. Develop Reinforcement Plan
XI. Deliver Training
XII. Perform Shared Tasks After Training Completed
XIII. Monitor the Measures
XIV. Provide Reinforcement
XV. Expand TPM Application
XVI. Implement Equipment Availability Improvement
XVII. Conclusion

Figure 5-1
TPM IMPLEMENTATION PLAN

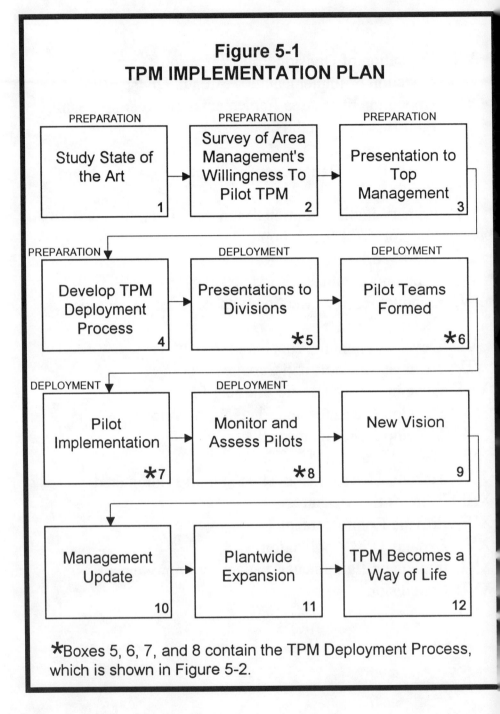

*Boxes 5, 6, 7, and 8 contain the TPM Deployment Process, which is shown in Figure 5-2.

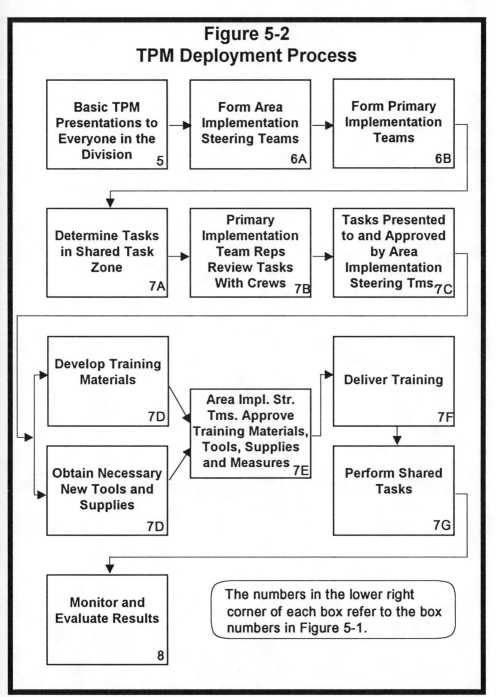

Figure 5-2
TPM Deployment Process

Basic TPM Presentations to Everyone in the Division 5

Form Area Implementation Steering Teams 6A

Form Primary Implementation Teams 6B

Determine Tasks in Shared Task Zone 7A

Primary Implementation Team Reps Review Tasks With Crews 7B

Tasks Presented to and Approved by Area Implementation Steering Tms 7C

Develop Training Materials 7D

Obtain Necessary New Tools and Supplies 7D

Area Impl. Str. Tms. Approve Training Materials, Tools, Supplies and Measures 7E

Deliver Training 7F

Perform Shared Tasks 7G

Monitor and Evaluate Results 8

The numbers in the lower right corner of each box refer to the box numbers in Figure 5-1.

6 How To Implement TPM - Preparation

Sections In This Chapter

I. Sell TPM and Gain Management's Commitment
    A. "Sales Pitch" Outline
    B. Explanation of "Sales Pitch" Outline
II. Feasibility Team
    A. Appointment and Membership
    B. Responsibilities of Feasibility Team
        1. Determine State of the Art
        2. Determine Current Culture - Your Locale
        3. Determine Readiness for TPM
        4. Other Feasibility Considerations
            a. Outline
            b. Explanation of Outline
        5. Make Recommendation to Management
III. Make Go/No Go Decision
IV. TPM Staff
    A. Appoint TPM Staff
    B. Develop TPM Implementation Plan
        (Figure 6-3)

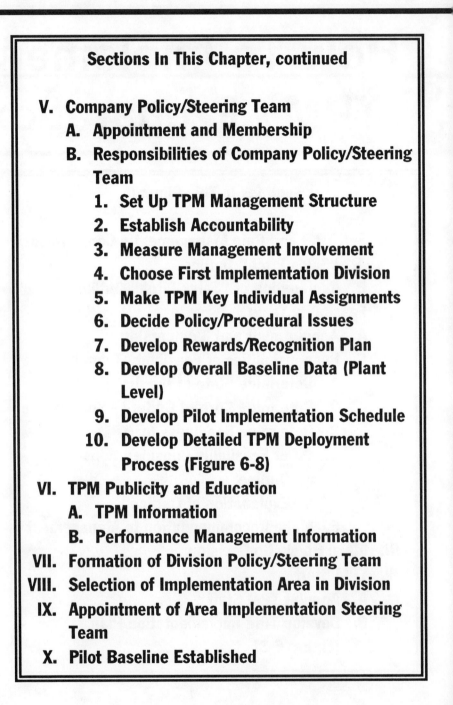

I. Sell TPM and Gain Management's Commitment

The first step in selling TPM is to gain management support. While this obviously means top management, it also includes all levels of management and supervision. Do not expect unanimous approval, especially at the beginning. First, strive for agreement that TPM is a worthwhile endeavor.

Although the initial selling effort will be directed at top management, you should begin the process of selling other levels of management at the same time. This generally involves giving TPM presentations to key managers in both Operations and Maintenance. Usually, you will make several presentations rather than just one or two. You should create a plan that will keep the TPM goals in front of these groups rather than a plan which offers a one-time explanation.

After you have the support of top management, do not take their continued support for granted. As you sell the rest of the organization, do not forget to keep in touch with this group. Until your results begin to show, you should keep them informed about TPM's progress.

If your organization decides to implement TPM, the selling effort must continue until TPM has become a way of life. This will not happen quickly and should never be taken for granted. No program, whether directed at quality, productivity, or maintenance, will thrive without a continual effort to keep it alive and productive. This means that people who have been sold on the concept and practice must keep in touch and be involved with the successes on an ongoing basis.

I. Sell TPM and Gain Management's Commitment (cont'd)
A. "Sales Pitch" Outline

A brief outline of your "sales pitch" for TPM might look something like this:

I. Define TPM
   A.   What it is
   B.   What it's not

II. Define the need for TPM
   A.   Top management level
      1. Long range reduced cost
      2. Culture change
         a. Employee involvement
         b. Emphasis on quality and safety
   B.   Operations management level
      1. Define potential output of operation
      2. Compare potential output to actual production
      3. Other benefits of TPM
   C.   Maintenance management level
      1. Relate maintenance work load to machine downtime
      2. Inappropriate use of skilled people to do low-skill jobs

3. Difficulty of scheduling preventive maintenance work due to emergencies

III. Present TPM as a solution to the need
  A. Explain the concept
    1. Emphasize benefits
    2. Show how TPM will meet the needs discussed earlier
  B. Use data from outside your organization to demonstrate
    1. Use track record of other industries (See Chapter 9, *TPM at Tennessee Eastman Division*)
      a. Number of people in the program
      b. Number of tasks transferred
      c. Improved employee morale
      d. Dollar savings
    2. Presentation at your site by a successful TPM group
    3. Visit another site where TPM is already implemented

I. Sell TPM and Gain Management's Commitment (cont'd)
B. Explanation of "Sales Pitch" Outline

Begin with a brief definition of TPM; also, tell what TPM is *NOT,* as discussed in Chapter 2. Next, discuss the need for TPM. Why do you need something different? The needs will vary with each level of management (top or middle) as well as each area of management (Operations or Maintenance). For top management, mention the 400% Return On Investment that is typical of TPM implementations. Emphasize the safety aspects of the TPM program and the empowerment of employees to do quality work.

For Operations management, showing the need will involve defining areas of opportunity for improvement. This can be done by defining the potential output of the operation and comparing it to the actual production. Your management's style of operation will determine how detailed and accurate you must be in this analysis.

Of course, TPM alone cannot help you achieve 100% of the potential improvement in output. Therefore, assign some percentage of this potential output improvement to improved machine uptime. When calculating this number, be sure to include the increased output that will result and the side benefits of this, such as reduced overtime for operators and mechanics. There are other benefits for which you may not be able to obtain actual numbers, such as reduced waste, reduced off-quality material, and improved ship-to-promise performance. These should be mentioned and calculated if possible.

For Maintenance management also, showing the need will relate to machine downtime. Usually, this is measured by the mechanics' work load, the inappropriate use of skilled personnel to perform low-skill jobs, and the difficulty in properly scheduling and performing preventive maintenance work because emergencies consume most of the mechanics' time.

When the need to change is recognized, TPM should be presented as the best solution.

> NOTE: Another solution would be a complete redesign of the whole work system -- an expensive process which is likely to be very unsettling to the workforce. A complete redesign would be revolution; TPM is evolution. A complete redesign would be imposed from the top down; TPM is implemented from the bottom up. The people do TPM; it is not done to them.

At this point, you should be prepared to explain the concept, emphasizing its benefits. (See Chapter 2, *What Is TPM?*, and Chapter 3, *Why Use TPM?*.) Show how TPM will meet the specific needs identified earlier. This usually involves describing the improvements TPM can provide, using supporting data. Until you have successes within your organization, this data must come from the outside. Fortunately, this data is plentiful from case histories at Tennessee Eastman Division, as discussed in Chapter 9 of this book. You may want to suggest having a presentation at your site by an outside TPM group, or else suggest a visit by key people from your organization to some other plant where TPM is already implemented.

When top management agrees at least to look at the possibility of implementing TPM, the next step is the formation of a Feasibility Team.

II. Feasibility Team
A. Appointment and Membership

As part of the total TPM team structure (see Chapter 4), top management should appoint a Feasibility Team. The typical members of a Feasibility Team are:

+ Company Maintenance Director
+ TPM Champion
+ Personnel Resources Representative
+ Operations Representatives
+ Maintenance Representatives

II. Feasibility Team (cont'd)
B. Responsibilities of Feasibility Team

The Feasibility Team is charged with doing a feasibility study to determine whether or not Total Productive Maintenance will be a success in your organization. The feasibility study, a more formal look at your organization's needs, attempts to generate hard numbers to guide your thinking. The five major tasks for the Feasibility Team are discussed in the following text.

II. Feasibility Team (cont'd)
B. Responsibilities of Feasibility Team (cont'd)
1. Determine State of the Art

Find out the state of the art in current TPM programs. This will include learning about the general aspects of the TPM program, but not the specific details of the training process. The Feasibility Team should learn how TPM functions in other companies. All or part of them may wish to travel to locations where TPM has been successfully implemented so that they can observe a current program. Or, they might want to have a presentation by a TPM group.

I. Feasibility Team (cont'd)
B. Responsibilities of Feasibility Team (cont'd)
2. Determine Current Culture - Your Locale

Determine the current culture in your organization. Before deciding to implement TPM, it is important to know the culture in your place of business. Before TPM can be implemented, the issues that concern your employees must first be addressed. At TED, we interviewed many employees about the possibility of piloting an effort to expand the skills of both operators and craftworkers at their daily interfaces. The following is a partial list of their concerns and/or fears about such a process:

Operators' Concerns and/or Fears

1. I'm Covered Up Already
2. People Will Get Hurt
3. More Work, Same Pay
4. Didn't Hire Me As A Mechanic
5. I'll Get Dirty And Contaminate The Product
6. Just Another Program

77

Mechanics' Concerns and/or Fears

1.   The Operators Will Get In Over Their Heads
2.   Operators Might Get Hurt
3.   They Want To Eliminate My Job
4.   The Equipment Will Fall Apart
5.   I Could Shut Down Something I Shouldn't

II. Feasibility Team (cont'd)
B. Responsibilities of Feasibility Team (cont'd)
3. Determine Readiness for TPM

Do a profile assessment for the whole plant, including the potential pilot area, to determine the readiness for TPM. A Profile Assessment form and the variables to consider when completing it are shown as Figure 6-1 and Figure 6-2. The Profile Assessment provided here is not the only way to evaluate your company. However, it provides a starting point in case you want to create your own evaluation system.

The purpose of the Profile Assessment is to help the Feasibility Team decide whether the organization as a whole is ready for TPM. Analysis of the Profile Assessment will provide four things: (1) detection of the company's weakest categories which because they are weak, need high priority work, (2) a comparison of the perceptions of the various groups (management, union, and others) and how well they agree, (3) an overall rating which indicates the company's readiness for TPM or not, and (4) ratings for individual areas in the company, showing which areas are the most likely candidates for initial TPM implementation.

If the Profile Assessment is done as a survey, the people who fill it out for your company should include a cross section of all employees, and not just management. Mechanics, operators, and first-line supervisors should be included. The survey should be conducted anonymously; however, each respondent should indicate his or her job function (an operator, a mechanic, a first-line supervisor, a staff person, union management, company management, or any other) and work area in the company. The Profile Assessment considers eight variables. It assigns a weight to each and assumes that you will judge how well your company performs in this area against a scale of 1 to 10. When you have rated each variable, multiply the point value times the rating to get your score. Add all eight scores to get a total. The maximum score possible is 1000. A total score of 700 or above indicates that your organization is ready for TPM. A score less than 500 indicates that you need to do some work in one or more areas before TPM will be successful. If your score is between 500 and 700, you should cautiously pilot a small TPM effort in the area with the greatest potential for success (i.e., the area with the highest score).

> NOTE: When a large organization is surveyed, the Profile Assessment frequently returns a score of around 500-600. This "average" score results from the large number of people and areas being

surveyed. However, within the large company, there will usually be "pockets of excellence" which will come to light as a result of the Profile Assessment. One of these areas with a higher score should be your first choice for a TPM pilot effort.

As the Feasibility Team members analyze the Profile Assessment data, they should look at the rating categories to determine the company's biggest weaknesses. If your management decides not to implement TPM at this time, the weak areas are where you need to direct your efforts to enhance future implementation of TPM. If your management decides to implement TPM now, the weak areas on the Profile Assessment are those that will probably give you trouble. Also, the Feasibility Team should look at the variability in responses to each category from the different groups. If management rates a particular category high and everyone else rates it low, then you know you have at least two major cultures in your organization. This situation needs to be addressed before you move ahead with TPM. For an example of a situation in which this type situation occurred, see Case History 6-A.

It is suggested that the results of the Profile Assessment be kept confidential until the Feasibility Team analyzes the results. (For additional comments about using the Profile Assessment in choosing the first (or pilot) TPM implementation area(s), see section V.D.4, "Choose First Implementation Division," in this chapter.)

Case History 6-A

We once worked with a company that sent its people to a TPM seminar in a large city from some distance away. The management people and the union people traveled together, stayed in the same hotel, and dined together; in the seminar, it was very difficult to tell who was management and who was union. However, when we started doing the Profile Assessment and asked about the management-union relationship (whether it was antagonistic or partnership-oriented), the union people rated the company a 3, while the management people rated it a 7. The true rating was probably not higher than 7 or lower than 3, but the difference was so great that they needed to ask themselves some questions: What is the difference? Do we have some under-the-surface trust issues to deal with? Are there some antagonistic feelings that need to be cleared up before we try to establish a TPM partnership?

Figure 6-1 - TPM PROFILE ASSESSMENT

VARIABLE	(1-10 RATING)	X (WEIGHT)	=SCORE
1. DOWNTIME LOSSES 1 ←————RATING————→ 10 SPARE CAPACITY / PRODUCTION SOLD OUT LOW DEMAND / LOTS OF LOSSES		25	
2. EQUIPMENT CHARACTERISTICS 1 ←————RATING————→ 10 EFFECTIVE PREVENTIVE / BREAKDOWNS OCCUR MAINTENANCE / FREQUENTLY		10	
3. DATA SYSTEMS 1 ←————RATING————→ 10 PERFORMANCE DATA IS / PERFORMANCE DATA DIFFICULT TO OBTAIN / IS EASILY OBTAINED		5	
4. STABILITY OF OPERATIONS 1 ←————RATING————→ 10 FREQUENT WORKER ROTATION / STABLE WORKLOAD HIGH EMPLOYEE TURNOVER / SKILLED, STABLE WORKFORCE		10	
5. AVAILABILITY OF RESOURCES 1 ←————RATING————→ 10 ONE MORE THING (SUCH AS / CAN GIVE TPM TPM) COULD BE TOO MUCH / TOP PRIORITY		10	
6. POSITIVE RELATIONSHIPS 1 ←————RATING————→ 10 GROUPS ARE ANTAGONISTIC / SUPPORTIVE, TRUSTING DEFENSIVE POSITIONS TAKEN / RELATIONSHIPS		20	
7. RECEPTIVITY TO CHANGE 1 ←————RATING————→ 10 ACTIVELY RESISTS CHANGE / OPEN TO CHANGE		10	
8. POTENTIAL IMPACT OF TPM 1 ←————RATING————→ 10 WILL BE DIFFICULT TO / SUBSTANTIAL ECONOMIC MEASURE ECONOMIC GAINS / GAINS TO BE MADE		10	
		TOTAL SCORE	

Figure 6-2
ADDITIONAL CONSIDERATIONS FOR COMPLETING THE TPM PROFILE ASSESSMENT

Use this expanded list of characteristics to help decide how to rate yourself on the TPM Profile Assessment (Figure 6-1). The more the following characteristics describe your organization, the higher your rating should be.

1. **DOWNTIME LOSSES**
   Product Sold Out
   High Demand For Product
   Much Waste
   Low Product Quality
   High Re-Start Costs
   Idled Personnel

2. **EQUIPMENT CHARACTERISTICS**
   Breakdowns Occur Frequently
   Complicated, Technical Equipment
   Remote Control
   Old Equipment
   High Amount Of Downtime
   Little Or No Preventive Maintenance

3. **DATA SYSTEMS**
   Performance Data Is Easily Obtained
   High Sophistication
   Have Ability To Measure Individual Performance
   Maintenance/Production Data Systems Are Integrated

Figure 6-2 (continued)
PROFILE ASSESSMENT CONSIDERATIONS

4. **STABILITY OF OPERATIONS**
   Stable Workload
   Skilled, Stable Workforce
   Operators Have Much Experience
   Few Equipment/Process Modifications

5. **AVAILABILITY OF RESOURCES**
   Other Programs Are Not Currently Competing For Resources
   Timing Good For Introduction Of TPM
   Can Meet TPM Time Requirements

6. **POSITIVE RELATIONSHIPS**
   Good Relationships Between:
   Supervision/Employees
   Operations/Maintenance
   Craft/Craft
   Company/Union
   Operations/Other Support Groups
   Maintenance/Other Support Groups

7. **RECEPTIVITY TO CHANGE**
   Operators Are Willing To Perform Maintenance Tasks
   Mechanics Are Willing To Perform Operator Tasks
   Supervisors Are Receptive To TPM
   Maintenance Group Endorses TPM

8. **POTENTIAL IMPACT OF TPM**
   Substantial Economic Gains To Be Made
   High Failure Frequency
   Downtime Loss Is A Problem
   High Maintenance Costs
   Maintenance Organization Has Receptive Point Of View
   Operations Organization Has Receptive Point Of View

II. Feasibility Team (cont'd)
B. Responsibilities of Feasibility Team (cont'd)
4. Other Feasibility Considerations

Consider the "who, what, where, and why" of TPM. The Feasibility Team must investigate many areas. The following outline, suggesting areas of possible investigation, is merely an attempt to get you started, and is not the only way to approach the issues. Your organization may require more or less than is indicated here.

II. Feasibility Team (cont'd)
B. Responsibilities of Feasibility Team (cont'd)
4. Other Feasibility Considerations (cont'd)
a. Outline of Other Feasibility Considerations

I. General Overview
  - A. General situation
  - B. Long range plans
  - C. Equipment investment plans
  - D. Equipment utilization approach

II. Quantifying the need
  - A. Define the capacity of the system
  - B. Determine the current output
  - C. Estimate value of losses due to:
    - 1. Machine downtime
    - 2. Idle time and overtime (production employees)

3. Machine-caused defects and waste

4. Repair costs (parts and labor)

5. Actual time vs. theoretical

III. Maintenance practices
  A. How are work orders processed?
  B. What percent of time is spent on emergency work?
  C. What is the state of preventive maintenance?
  D. Analyze reasons for downtime
  E. Organizational practices (managing crafts)

IV. Receptivity of the people
  A. Management practices pertaining to the people
  B. Employee involvement practices
  C. Employee receptivity to change
  D. Union leadership acceptance
  E. Past practices on craft jurisdictional lines

 V. Stability of the workforce
  A. Longevity of crews and mechanics
  B. Skill level (operators and craftworkers)
  C. Turnover

VI. Organizational resources
  A. Availability of champion and facilitator
  B. Management time devoted to TPM
  C. Ability to train new employees in TPM skills
  D. Ability to track TPM data

VII. Management practices
    A. Confrontational vs. Collaborative
    B. Participative (open to teams?)
    C. Supervisory-employee relations
    D. Union cooperation

VIII. Calculations
    A. Estimated return
    B. Estimated costs
    C. Return on investment

IX. Recommendations

I. Feasibility Team (cont'd)
B. Responsibilities of Feasibility Team (cont'd)
4. Other Feasibility Considerations (cont'd)
b. Explanation of Outline

After you have completed a general look at where your organization is and where it wants to go (Section I of the preceding outline), you must determine the extent of the need for change (Section II). This is done by looking at the potential for improving performance. Obviously, the focus will be on the contribution which better maintenance will make. The numbers obtained here relating to production and machine run time will be valuable to you later; therefore, you will save time during subsequent phases if you do thorough calculations at this point.

87

In determining this need, be sure to include the following points. equipment availability/reliability, labor productivity, product quality, and waste. For most organizations these will form the basis of your decision. TPM is a "hard dollars" approach to reducing production costs and increasing output. Even in organizations where management does not consider this to be the most important outcome, the longevity of the TPM program will depend on management's being able to see ongoing cost benefits.

Next (section III of the outline), you should examine the ability of the Maintenance organization to fully meet its requirements. You should let it be known that this study is not intended to point out a "guilty" party, but instead to provide an objective look at your resources and performance. Of particular interest will be the age and condition of the equipment, an analysis of downtime, an understanding of how both routine and emergency work are done, and the current level of preventive maintenance. You should also look at the structure of the Maintenance organization. Are multiple crafts present? How rigid are the precedents which define what one craft will or will not do?

Another area of investigation should be the culture of the units where TPM will be introduced (IV). What are the characteristics of the management approach with regard to the people and their work? Would you characterize the relationship between managers and their supervisors and their employees as being supportive? Is there a reservoir of trust and good will? Is employee involvement apparent? Is there a sense of team spirit?

How open have both management and employees been to past change initiatives? Is the level of interest in programs that will improve performance an asset or liability?

The more stable a work force (V), the greater the long-term benefit from TPM. Turnover presents a challenge to supervision because training of new employees in TPM methods is less likely to be maintained. Also, high training costs decrease the cost savings from TPM implementation.

The Feasibility Team should consider management's commitment of organizational resources (VI) and determine the time and effort that a TPM investment will require. This refers to the management *effort*, not the cost. A look at past quality and productivity initiatives will give you a starting point. Does management commit the necessary people and time to make programs work over the long term?

The section on management practices (VII) asks how well management has prepared the way for new programs. Performance Management is an integral part of the TPM process. It involves the delivery of positive reinforcement to all who perform the tasks and duties of TPM. Is employee reinforcement compatible with either the past practices or desires of management?

The calculations (VIII) of return on investment should be as accurate as your management desires. This will form the basis of evaluation for TPM's effectiveness and should be done with care. Be sure to document the assumptions on which you base these numbers.

II. Feasibility Team (cont'd)
B. Responsibilities of Feasibility Team (cont'd)
5. Make Recommendation to Management

Make a recommendation to company management. Your recommendation to implement TPM or not will take into consideration any facts you may have discovered, whether or not they are included in the above outline. These facts should be cited so you may return to them later.

After the findings of the Feasibility Team are presented, top management should decide whether to implement TPM or not.

III. Make Go/No Go Decision

Will you implement TPM? Top management will make one of the following decisions:

- ► Yes, we will implement TPM plantwide.
- ► We will pilot TPM in two or three areas first, then decide whether or not to implement it plantwide.
- ► No, we won't have TPM at this time.

Once the decision is made by top management, the Feasibility Team is disbanded. If top management decides to go ahead with

TPM, some or all of the Feasibility Team members should be assigned to the Company Policy/Steering Team (See Section V., "Company Policy/Steering Team").

IV. TPM Staff
A. Appoint TPM Staff

Top management should appoint the TPM staff, which will include a TPM Manager and some TPM Coordinators. For these people, TPM implementation will be their whole job. They are charged with providing consistency to the process throughout the organization. One or more members of the TPM staff will meet with each Steering team and each Primary Implementation Team, every time they meet. For a complete list of the TPM Coordinator's responsibilities, see the latter pages of Chapter 6 and all of Chapter 7; find the "TPM Coordinator's Check List" boxes. Each section containing a "TPM Coordinator's Check List" box is designated with an arrow (➡).

IV. TPM Staff (cont'd)
B. Develop TPM Implementation Plan (Figure 6-3)

Soon after their appointment, the TPM Staff should develop a proposed Implementation Plan. The Implementation Plan is not a detailed, step-by-step process for every facet of TPM Implementation. It is, instead, an overall plan for introduction and implementation of TPM in your company, whatever its size. A sample Implementation Plan is shown in Figure 6-3.

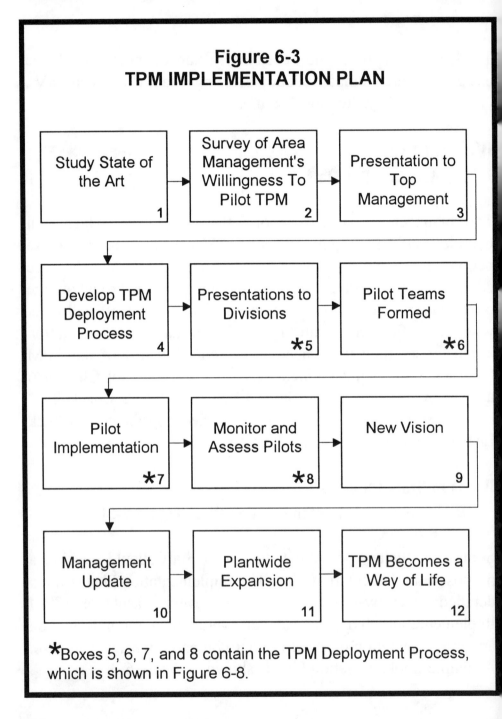

Figure 6-3
TPM IMPLEMENTATION PLAN

*Boxes 5, 6, 7, and 8 contain the TPM Deployment Process, which is shown in Figure 6-8.

V. Company Policy/Steering Team
A. Appointment and Membership

This team may include some or all of the members of the Feasibility Team; additional people may also be needed. The Company Policy/Steering Team should include not just manufacturing and maintenance representatives, but also human resources personnel, since pay issues must be addressed. A typical Company Policy/Steering Team might include the following people:

* TPM Manager
* Company Maintenance Director
* Human Resources Representative
* An Operating Division Director
* A Maintenance Department Superintendent
* An Operating Department Superintendent

V. Company Policy/Steering Team (cont'd)
B. Responsibilities of Company Policy/Steering Team

The role of this team is to ensure that policy and procedural issues concerning the implementation of TPM are resolved. The seven major tasks for this team are listed below. Under each task, policy questions regarding that task are listed and explained.

V. Company Policy/Steering Team (cont'd)
B. Responsibilities of Company Policy/Steering Team (cont'd)
1. Set Up TPM Management Structure

Set up a management structure. All levels of management should be involved with the TPM process in some active, meaningful way that is not intensive or time-consuming. As mentioned earlier, TPM is driven from the bottom up. However, only management can create the vision and define success for the process and for the organization.

The management structure of TPM will vary with the size of your organization. For example, if your company employs 65 people, then you might have one team that would function as the Feasibility Team, the Company Policy/Steering Team, and the Area Implementation Steering Team. There might be two or three Primary Implementation teams reporting to the Feasibility/Policy/Steering Team. (See Figure 6-4.) However, if yours is a large corporation, you might have a corporate Feasibility Team, a corporate Policy/Steering Team, a Company Policy/Steering Team at each plant site, several Division Policy/Steering Teams at each plant site, an Area Implementation Steering Team in each department of each division, and several Primary Implementation Teams reporting to each Area Implementation Steering Team. (See Figure 6-5.)

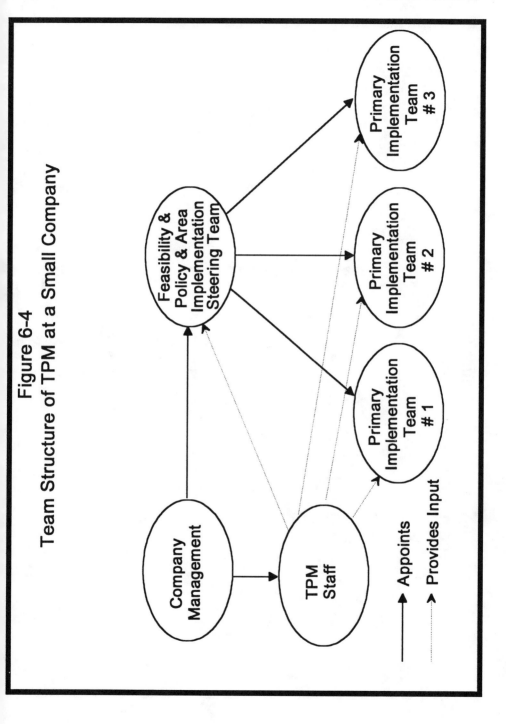

Figure 6-4
Team Structure of TPM at a Small Company

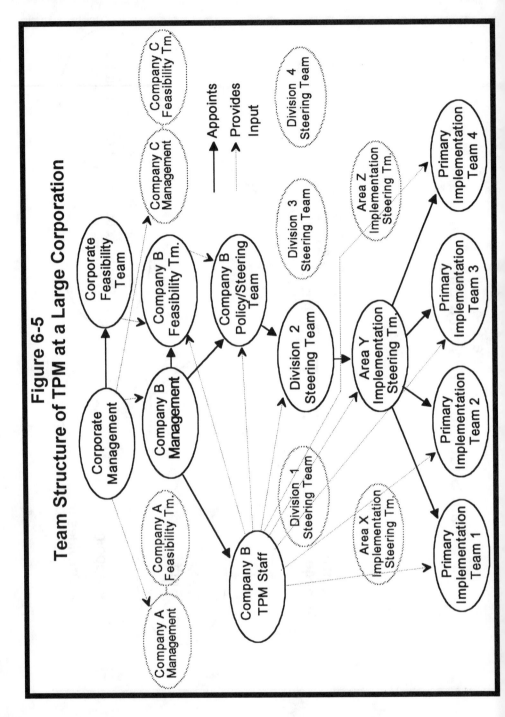

Figure 6-5
Team Structure of TPM at a Large Corporation

Design your TPM management structure so that all levels of management are involved in supporting and reinforcing the TPM effort but are not involved in managing the TPM Primary Implementation Teams. (See also Chapter 4, *Team Structure of TPM*.)

The Company Policy/Steering Team should consider these questions:

- Will we use team management?
- Will we have a dedicated TPM manager (i.e., will TPM responsibilities be the manager's only job?)?
- During implementation in a particular area, will the Primary Implementation Team Leader be assigned only to TPM?
- Will we have Division TPM Policy/Steering Teams? Department TPM Steering Teams? Area TPM Implementation Steering Teams? Primary Implementation Teams?
- What will be the levels and/or disciplines represented on the teams?
- What will be the role of each team?
- Will we have a TPM Company Policy/Steering Team?
- Will we have Division TPM Policy/Steering Teams? Department TPM Steering Teams? Area TPM Implementation Steering Teams? Primary Implementation Teams?
- What will be the levels and/or disciplines represented on the teams?
- What will be the role of each team?

V. Company Policy/Steering Team (cont'd)
B. Responsibilities of Company Policy/Steering Team (cont'd)
2. Establish Accountability

Establish accountability for all those who should be participating. Individuals who become involved with TPM should have an active role to play. Where individuals have authority but no role, they are usually placed in the position where their main reinforcement comes from playing the devil's advocate. This frequently leads to the individual's taking an oppositional stance to TPM. If you are to be as successful as possible with TPM, you must be able to define for each person which supportive behaviors and results will earn them the most reinforcement.

The Company Policy/Steering Team should consider this question:

- What will be the roles of key TPM players?

V. Company Policy/Steering Team (cont'd)
B. Responsibilities of Company Policy/Steering Team (cont'd)
3. Measure Management Involvement

Measure management involvement. There are several tasks that only management can perform. Management should determine how to measure its own progress in support of TPM implementation.

The Company Policy/Steering Team should consider these questions:

- ✦ What are the milestones for management?
- ✦ What forms will we use to collect data on management involvement?
- ✦ What is our plan for collecting, analyzing, and distributing this data?
- ✦ Who will do the data analysis and generate the reports?

V. Company Policy/Steering Team (cont'd)
B. Responsibilities of Company Policy/Steering Team (cont'd)
4. Choose First Implementation Division

Conduct a TPM Profile Assessment of several areas in order to determine where to introduce TPM first. There is a tendency in some organizations to start TPM in an area which needs it the most. However, you must be careful that the introduction of TPM does not become a signal that a particular area is in trouble. This will only increase the resistance you get from the initial and subsequent pilots. The recommended approach is to begin TPM in an area where conditions are most favorable for success. Starting with areas which are among your best will facilitate TPM's introduction to the areas which need it most. Completion of the Profile Assessment will help determine which area is best prepared, which people are willing to try TPM, and who will be the champions (those people who are really enthused about TPM) in the pilot area.

A manufacturing unit involved with TPM should experience an increase in positive reinforcement. Therefore, you want to find a unit which tends to be positive and supportive in its approach to people. Where distrust and strained relations between supervision and employees exist, you must do more preparation to ensure TPM's success. The introduction of TPM will help you improve these relations, but the distrust will slow the process down. You will see that the speed of implementation is directly influenced by the employee-supervisor relationships. The better they are, the faster you will progress.

The Profile Assessment in Figure 6-1 is not the only way to evaluate your units. However, it provides a starting point in case you want to create your own evaluation system.

The Profile Assessment considers eight variables. It assigns a weight to each and assumes that you will judge how well the unit performs in this area against a scale of 1 to 10. When you have rated each variable, multiply the point value times the rating to get your score. Add all eight scores to get a total. The maximum score possible is 1000.

It is suggested that the results of the Profile Assessments be kept confidential until they have been thoroughly analyzed. The purpose of this survey is to determine the need for, and the probability of success of, Total Productive Maintenance. The lower the score, the greater the need; the higher the score, the greater the probability of success. The Profile Assessment is not an appropriate instrument for either reinforcement or punishment. If the scores are made known, the potential for perceived punishment is great. People who are punished become less open to new ideas and to change, which are the very substance of TPM. While such a situation would not prevent the successful implementation of TPM, it would make implementation more difficult, and thus, more costly. The potential for reinforcement for those groups having a high score is not great enough to offset the cost of punishment for the groups having a low score.

The Company Policy/Steering Team should consider the following questions:

- Will we have a pilot implementation?
- Which unit will be chosen for the pilot implementation? The following criteria should describe the first implementation area:
    - Good operations/maintenance relationship
    - Receptive operations/maintenance management
    - Receptive operators and mechanics
    - Stable operation
    - Available task opportunities
    - Employees have good knowledge of process

101

- • A natural community within a manufacturing module, with all employees having a commonality and constancy of purpose
- ♦ Will pilot teams have the right to reverse their recommendations?

V. Company Policy/Steering Team (cont'd)
B. Responsibilities of Company Policy/Steering Team (cont'd)
5. Make TPM Key Individual Assignments

Select individuals to fill TPM assignments. Several of the TPM roles which are critical to the process need special attention. The Primary Implementation Team Leaders must be chosen with great care. Selection criteria should be developed which will ensure that those chosen are high performers with good interpersonal skills.

The Company Policy/Steering Team should consider the following questions:

- ♦ Who will be the TPM Manager? What will be the TPM Manager's background? To whom will the TPM Manager report?
- ♦ Who will be on the TPM Manager's staff?
- ♦ Who will be the Area Implementation Steering Team Leader in the pilot area? This person should have the following characteristics:

- Enthusiastic and loyal employee
- Supporter of TPM
- Good leader and organizer
- Good team player
- Promotes use of data to manage
- Good knowledge of area from operations and maintenance viewpoint
- Flexible -- not bound by traditional approach
- Who will be the Primary Implementation Team Leader in the pilot area? This person should have the following characteristics:
  - Enthusiastic and loyal employee
  - Supporter of change
  - Good leader and organizer
  - Good team player
  - Good knowledge of pilot area from operations and maintenance viewpoint
  - Flexible -- not bound by traditional approach

V. Company Policy/Steering Team (cont'd)
B. Responsibilities of Company Policy/Steering Team (cont'd)
6. Decide Policy/Procedural Issues

Decide other policy/procedural issues. Some of the predictable issues are listed below. A brainstorming session with the managers involved in the TPM implementation will quickly generate a list of concerns and identify specific organizational questions which need resolution. The goal is to make sure that the major issues have been addressed up front before TPM is presented to the Primary Implementation Teams (the people who actually do the work). You can count on people to ask about pay policies; if you don't have one, implementation will be stopped until you do.

The Company Policy/Steering Team should consider these questions:

+ Will we pay for skills? See Figure 6-6 for a sample pay policy.

Figure 6-6
Example Pay Policy

While TPM is expected to change the role of both operating and maintenance personnel, individual job classifications will normally not be affected by the types of duties which TPM Teams are likely to identify for reassignment. When performance of TPM tasks clearly affects the level of responsibility in a job assignment, management will request a study by Personnel Resources to determine if job classification/ level changes are required to meet established company pay policies. Such reviews should only be made after TPM has been implemented and transfer of tasks has occurred.

- Will we have local storerooms for tools or centralized stores? How will supplies at the job site be handled? Many companies today have centralized stores to reduce inventory. However, TPM requires that tools and supplies needed for TPM tasks be available at the job site. A policy is needed to provide tools and supplies at the job site. See Figure 6-7 for a sample tool policy.
- Will we train on overtime or during regular working hours? The policy here might state that training will depend on each particular area's Implementation Steering Team recommendation.
- Will trainers receive additional pay?
- Will trainees receive additional pay?
- What will the TPM charge codes be?
- Will we do task analysis and time saving calculations? (See Chapter 7, Figures 7-1, 7-2, and 7-3, for examples of worksheets.)
- Who will be responsible for developing each implementation area's measures?
- How will we monitor the TPM efforts?
- Will we have a strong emphasis on safety?
- Will we have promotion/education on TPM prior to our first Primary Implementation Team meeting? Will operators train mechanics and mechanics train operators?
- Will TPM be structured so that all employees in an area participate (take training and do the tasks) once the Primary Implementation Teams identify the tasks and the Implementation Steering Team approves them?

* Will tasks be identified at the organizational level that will be performing the tasks (i.e., by the Primary Implementation Team)?
* What will be our specific implementation process?
* What will be the long range plan for TPM?

V. Company Policy/Steering Team (cont'd)
B. Responsibilities of Company Policy/Steering Team (cont'd)
7. Develop Rewards/Recognition Plan

Develop a rewards/recognition plan for the members of all TPM teams. TPM's ultimate effectiveness resides in the willingness of management and employees to give discretionary effort -- to "go the extra mile." This willingness can be achieved best through positive reinforcement, which will occur frequently enough only if it is a managed activity. The rewards/recognition plan will ensure a consistent effort at managing the correct behaviors and results.

The Company Policy/Steering Team should consider the following question:

* What will be our rewards/recognition plan? The recommended plan is Performance Management, which motivates people not from pay, but from job satisfaction. See Chapter 8, *Reinforcement*.

Figure 6-7
Example Tool Procedure

I. Purpose

The purpose of this procedure is to establish a policy for the procurement and maintenance of tools to support the Total Productive Maintenance program (TPM) at (company name).

II. Policy

It is the intent of the Maintenance Division, working with operating departments, to furnish the initial tools required to perform TPM tasks. Operating departments will then be responsible for maintaining and replacing tools. Tools belong to the company and are not the personal property of operators.

III. Guidelines

1. Tool lists: A list of tools required to perform TPM tasks will be developed by the TPM Area Implementation Steering Team and TPM trainers.

2. Approval: The TPM Area Implementation Steering Team will approve the recommended tools.

3. Requisitions: Purchase requisitions will be prepared by the TPM Primary Implementation Team Leader and approved by the operating department and a TPM staff member.

4. Identification: The TPM Primary Implementation Team Leader will be responsible for seeing that all initial TPM tools are marked. Maintaining and procuring replacement tools will be the responsibility of the operating department.

5. TPM Expansion: Tools required to support TPM expansion will be purchased as outlined in Steps 1 through 4.

V. Company Policy/Steering Team (cont'd)
B. Responsibilities of Company Policy/Steering Team (cont'd)
8. Develop Overall Baseline Data (Plant Level)

Develop overall baseline data at the plant level. The Company Policy/Steering Team should consider the following question:

* By what criteria will we measure TPM's success?

V. Company Policy/Steering Team (cont'd)
B. Responsibilities of Company Policy/Steering Team (cont'd)
9. Develop Pilot Implementation Schedule

Develop a pilot implementation schedule. The Company Policy/Steering Team should consider the following questions:

* If there are to be pilot areas, which ones are they? Which one will be first, second, etc.?
* If TPM is to be implemented across the entire organization without a pilot, where will the first implementation take place? (You can't do it everywhere at once because of the time requirements for your TPM staff.)

V. Company Policy/Steering Team (cont'd)

B. Responsibilities of Company Policy/Steering Team (cont'd)

10. Develop Detailed TPM Deployment Process

Develop a detailed TPM Deployment Process. A TPM Deployment Process should be developed by the Company Policy/Steering Team working with the TPM staff. This process is to be used in each area where TPM is implemented. A suggested Deployment Process is shown in Figure 6-8.

After its tasks are completed, the Company Policy/Steering Team may not need to meet again on a regular basis. However, it should always exist and be ready to meet on as as-needed basis to decide matters of policy that may arise in subsequent areas of TPM implementation.

VI. TPM Publicity and Education

NOTE: Sections marked with an arrow (➡) indicate the implementation steps for which the TPM Coordinator has some or all of the responsibility.

A. TPM Information

You (the TPM Coordinator for the area) and the TPM Staff should go into the proposed pilot implementation area and hold

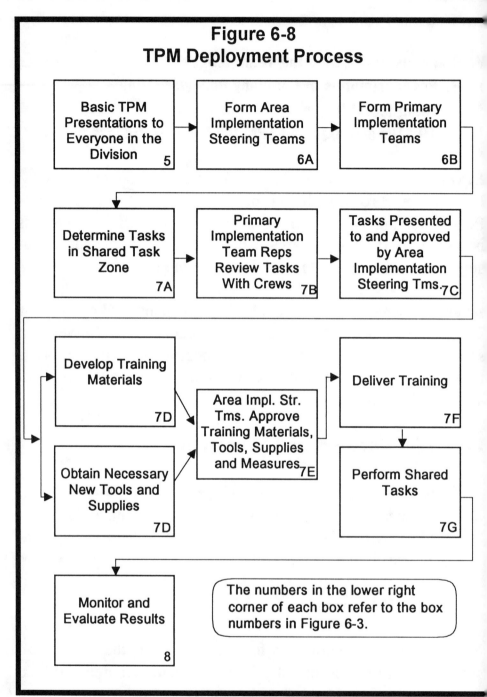

Figure 6-8
TPM Deployment Process

one-on-one meetings with key operations and maintenance management personnel. Explain the TPM culture (see Figure 6-9), tell them that company management has decided to implement TPM on a pilot basis, and tell them that they have the opportunity to be a part of the program. Explain that it is a pilot effort, stating that the decision to use TPM is not final. Clearly explain that just because a division pilots TPM doesn't mean that it will definitely be implemented long-term. If the division management approves implementing TPM, tell them that you

Figure 6-9
The TPM Culture

► Forms a partnership between operations and maintenance
► Develops teamwork among all levels of employees
► Creates a willingness to do what needs to be done

would like to publicize TPM in the division and that you would like for them to discuss TPM in their natural unit teams. (The division management may ask you to come to the natural unit team meetings to further explain TPM. Do it.) Explain to division management that they will need to appoint a division TPM steering team and that they will have ample opportunity to ask questions and voice their concerns before they try TPM. You should expect questions about pay and be prepared to answer them based on decisions made by the Company Policy/Steering Team.

If your organization does not have Team Management, Quality Management, Performance Management, and/or Statistical Process Control, don't use these terms to explain TPM. Explain TPM so that the people who will be involved in it will understand it.

If a particular division decides not to have TPM, then don't push the issue any further. If they don't want TPM, it should not be forced on them. Another pilot area should be selected, and the group that refused should be offered the opportunity again at a later date, after other TPM successes.

VI. TPM Publicity and Education (cont'd)
B. Performance Management Information

This book recommends Performance Management as the motivational tool to be used with TPM implementation. Performance Management is a tool which Tennessee Eastman Division and many other organizations have used with great success; it is based on industrial psychology and includes the elements of goals, feedback, and reinforcement. Employees are motivated from a sense of job satisfaction, not from additional pay.

If your operations and maintenance management personnel are not familiar with Performance Management, tell them what it is and give a brief explanation. Chapter 8 contains information about Performance Management and shows how it has been used in reinforcing employees who are participating in TPM.

Performance Management is recommended. However, if you are in a union atmosphere, negotiations may need to take place to pay your employees for doing the TPM tasks. Keep in mind, though, that additional pay will add to the cost for TPM and make it harder to justify on a cost savings basis.

TPM Coordinator's Check List
Step 1: TPM Publicity and Education

☐ TPM and PM Presentations to Key Operations Personnel
☐ TPM and PM Presentations to Key Maintenance Personnel

VII. Formation of Division Policy/Steering Team

After division management agrees to try TPM, their next step is to appoint the Division TPM Policy/Steering Team. This team should have the following membership:

+ Operations Division Director
+ Operating Department Superintendent(s)
+ Company Maintenance Director
+ Maintenance Department Superintendent(s)
+ TPM Manager
+ TPM Coordinator(s)

113

Please see Chapter 4, *Team Structure of TPM*, for a list of this team's responsibilities.

```
┌─────────────────────────────────────────────────────┐
│                                                       │
│              TPM Coordinator's Check List             │
│      Step 2: Division Policy/Steering Team Formed      │
│                                                       │
│   ☐ Operations Representatives                         │
│   ☐ Maintenance Representatives                        │
│   ☐ TPM Coordinator Assigned                          │
│   ☐ Team Responsibilities Established                  │
│                                                       │
└─────────────────────────────────────────────────────┘
```

➤VIII. Selection of Implementation Area in Division

The Division Policy/Steering Team should now select the first area which will implement TPM in the division. Remind them that it is best to implement TPM first in an area with strong employee relations, and not in a "problem" area. Attention should be given to any conditions or situations which are specific to the area and may affect TPM implementation, such as particularly hazardous materials, handicapped employees, complicated processes, etc. One of the major factors to consider in selecting the first effort is the desire and commitment of the area's management.

After the first implementation area within the division is selected, you (the TPM Coordinator) and TPM Staff should go into the proposed pilot implementation area and hold meetings with every crew.

Explain the TPM culture (see Figure 6-9), say that company management has decided to implement TPM on a pilot basis, and tell them that they have the opportunity to be a part of the program. Explain that it is a pilot effort and that the decision to use TPM has not been irrevocably made. Further explain that just because the crew pilots TPM doesn't mean that it will definitely be implemented long-term. Tell them that a Division Policy/Steering Team has been formed and that they will have ample opportunity to ask questions and voice their concerns before they try TPM. You should expect questions about pay and be prepared to answer them based on decisions made by the Company Policy/Steering Team.

If your organization does not have Team Management, Quality Management, Performance Management, and/or Statistical Process Control, don't use these terms to explain TPM. Explain TPM so that the people who will be involved in it will understand it.

Plan to go any time of day to give these informational presentations -- mornings, evenings, weekends -- whenever it is convenient for the crew, not necessarily for you.

As TPM is implemented throughout a particular area, one of the Primary Implementation Team Leaders will probably develop into the person who goes out to the crews to explain TPM and answer questions. TPM will most likely be better received if an insider explains it rather than an outsider. However, the TPM Staff should always be available to answer questions and clarify policy issues which have been decided by the Company Policy/Steering Team.

If a particular crew says they don't want to have TPM, then don't push the issue. If they don't want TPM, it should not be forced on them. Another pilot area should be selected, and the group that refused should be offered the opportunity again at a later date, after other TPM successes.

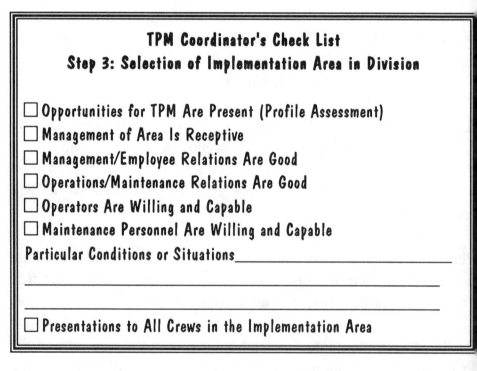

TPM Coordinator's Check List
Step 3: Selection of Implementation Area in Division

☐ Opportunities for TPM Are Present (Profile Assessment)
☐ Management of Area Is Receptive
☐ Management/Employee Relations Are Good
☐ Operations/Maintenance Relations Are Good
☐ Operators Are Willing and Capable
☐ Maintenance Personnel Are Willing and Capable
Particular Conditions or Situations_____
_____
_____
☐ Presentations to All Crews in the Implementation Area

X. Appointment of Area Implementation Steering Team

After all crews have heard presentations explaining TPM, the Area Implementation Steering Team should be appointed by the Division Policy/Steering Team. The Area Implementation Steering Team should include the following people:

* Area Engineer, Operations (Team Leader)
* General Supervisor, Maintenance
* Operations Supervisor
* Maintenance Supervisor
* Area Industrial Engineer
* TPM Trainers (ad hoc)
* TPM Coordinator

TPM Coordinator's Check List
Step 4: Appointment of Area Implementation Steering Team

☐ Operations Representatives
☐ Maintenance Representatives
☐ TPM Coordinator(s)
☐ Other Representatives
☐ Team Responsibilities Established
☐ TPM Presentation to All Members
☐ TPM Charge Codes Explained

➡X.   Pilot Baseline Established

At this point in the preparation phase, the Area Implementation
Steering Team needs to decide exactly what will be measured. In
order to deliver effective, sincere, positive reinforcement, you
must have accurate ways to measure the performance of your
TPM personnel. The following quote from Lord Kelvin
illustrates TPM's need for accurate measures of performance.

> "When you can measure what you are speaking about,
> and express it in numbers, you know something about
> it; but when you cannot measure it, when you cannot
> express it in numbers, your knowledge is of a meager
> and unsatisfactory kind."
>
> **Lord Kelvin, 1883**

You will need accurate baseline data against which you can
compare your TPM results. (Baseline data refers to conditions
existing before TPM implementation.) You may be able to use
numbers developed in the Feasibility Study to provide you with a
measure of how things were before TPM; however, this may not
work in every case. Some data is heavily influenced by factors
such as depreciation, tax considerations, or other financial
decisions. In these cases, it is best to use only the data which
reflects performance. It is improper to measure people or
organizations on measures which are beyond their control.

f your TPM implementation involves only a fraction of your total operation, the measures of success should be small unit measures. Rather than looking at Total Plant Productivity, consider Department Productivity instead. The issues are control and positive reinforcement. Do the TPM participants have control over the data you are measuring? Can you present the data in such a way that they will be positively reinforced when TPM produces positive results?

For the three TPM pilot efforts at Tennessee Eastman, the following items were measured:

* TPM Tasks Implemented
* Labor Hours Saved
* Cost Reduction
* Safety Performance

Case History 6-B

Crew 1390 at Tennessee Eastman measured the number of idler gears which failed (per week) and therefore required replacement. Figure 6-10 shows that, before TPM, the number was more than 60 per week. After TPM implementation, their goal of 10 replacements per week was soon met.

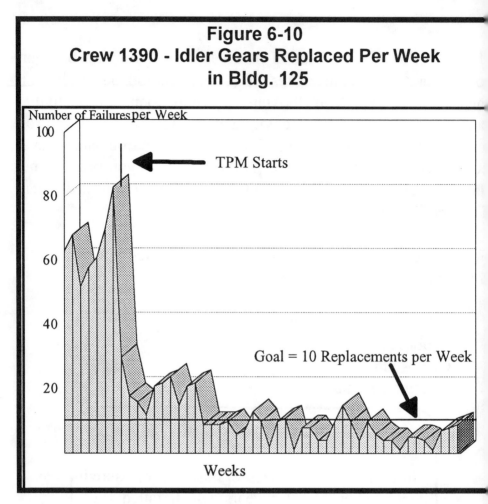

Figure 6-10
Crew 1390 - Idler Gears Replaced Per Week
in Bldg. 125

Number of Failures per Week

TPM Starts

Goal = 10 Replacements per Week

Weeks

Other examples of specific measurements used at Tennessee Eastman are:

- Crew 4390 measured Tow Feeder Oil Leaks per week
- Building 13 measured routine Maintenance and Repair Labor
- Building 13 measured the number of "After Hours" calls

* Building 13 measured the number of rupture disc failures per week
* A Power Distribution & Control Systems area measured the number of troubleshooting calls

Two other questions merit your consideration at this point: Who will be responsible for collecting the data on an on-going basis? How will this data be captured? Data that is difficult to compile and compute will present a continuing problem. Either simplify the process or the measures. Be sure the person designated to administer the system is reinforced when the job is done well.

TPM Coordinator's Check List
Step 5: Pilot Baseline Established

☐ Division Policy/Steering Team Establishes Measures
☐ Measures Are Meaningful to TPM Participants
☐ Data Collection Is Simple Process
☐ Person Assigned to Collect Data

In the next chapter, the actual deployment of TPM will be discussed.

7 How To Implement TPM - Deployment

Sections In This Chapter

I. Primary Implementation Team Appointed
II. Plan for TPM Workshop
III. TPM Workshop
IV. Summarize and Publish Workshop Results
V. Conduct Review Meeting with Area Implementation Steering Team
VI. Develop Training Procedures
VII. Arrange for Tools and Supplies
VIII. Develop Area-Specific Training Plan
IX. Develop Measures and Plans for Monitoring
X. Develop Reinforcement Plan
XI. Deliver Training
XII. Perform Shared Tasks After Training Completed
XIII. Monitor Measures
XIV. Provide Reinforcement
XV. Expand TPM Application
XVI. Implement Equipment Availability Improvement
XVII. Conclusion

►I. Primary Implementation Team Appointed

NOTE: An arrow (➡) designates the steps for which the TPM Coordinator has some or all of the responsibility.

The Area Implementation Steering Team should appoint the Primary Implementation Team. The major task of the Primary Implementation Team will be to determine which tasks are candidates for transfer. The leader of this team should be dedicated to TPM implementation; i.e., TPM should be his or her only job assignment. All groups should be represented on the Primary Implementation Team -- operators, mechanics, day people, shift people, and any others which you may have.

After the Primary Implementation Team has been appointed, all members have been notified, and TPM presentations have been given to every crew in the pilot area, start to publicize TPM throughout your entire organization. Be sure that the TPM participants in the pilot area have been informed before you start publicity. Briefly explain TPM and tell which areas will pilot it first.   Emphasize the aspects of machine uptime, maintenance/operations cooperation, and the elimination of barriers between these two groups. Use the company newsletter and bulletin boards.

```
┌────────────────────────────────────────────────────┐
│                                                      │
│              TPM Coordinator's Check List            │
│      Step 6: Primary Implementation Team Appointed   │
│                                                      │
│  ☐ Dedicated Team Leader (TPM Is Assignment)         │
│  ☐ Team Represents Entire Cross-Section              │
│     • Operators                                      │
│     • Mechanics (Area, Days, and Shifts)             │
│     • Control System Mechanics (Area, Shift Services, Days, and │
│       Shifts)                                        │
│     • Lubricators                                    │
│     • Other Service Group Representatives            │
│  ☐ TPM Coordinator Assigned                          │
│  ☐ All Team Members Formally Notified                │
│  ☐ TPM Presentations to All Crews (Maintenance/Operations) Before │
│     TPM Workshop                                     │
│  ☐ Workshop Scheduled (Date, Time, Place)            │
│  ☐ TPM Publicity Across the Organization             │
│                                                      │
└────────────────────────────────────────────────────┘
```

II. Plan for TPM Workshop

The TPM workshop is the meeting at which the Primary Implementation Team will identify the potential tasks for transfer, do task analysis using the Task Analysis Worksheets, and select the TPM tasks. If you have not already done so, be sure the Primary Implementation Team Leader has the TPM charge codes and is prepared to give them to the other members of the team. Your charge codes should be set up so that operations personnel can charge time to your maintenance program.

TPM Coordinator's Check List
Step 7: Plan for TPM Workshop

- ☐ Refreshments Scheduled
- ☐ Facilities, Equipment, and Supplies Scheduled
- ☐ Maintenance and Operations Speakers Arranged
- ☐ Agenda Developed
- ☐ Charge Codes to TPM Primary Implementation Team Leader
- ☐ Team Leader and TPM Coordinator Roles Reviewed
- ☐ Room Set Up

➔III. TPM Workshop

At the TPM Workshop, start with a *brief* review of TPM and the Primary Implementation Team responsibilities. Lead the team through brainstorming of TPM task opportunities and completion of the Task Analysis Sheets and the Time Savings Worksheets (Figures 7-1, 7-2, and 7-3). By the end of the workshop, you should have a list of proposed TPM tasks which will be presented to the Area Implementation Steering Team. If necessary, schedule another workshop to complete the task analysis.

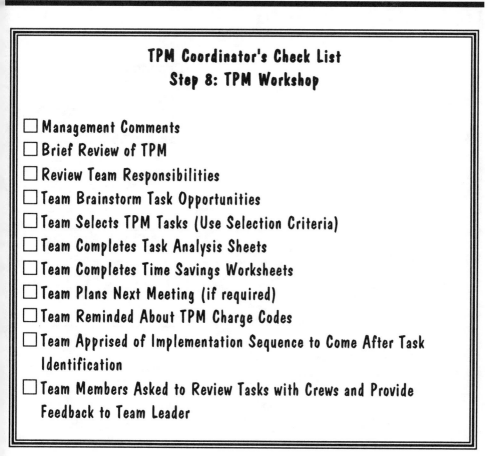

TPM Coordinator's Check List
Step 8: TPM Workshop

☐ Management Comments
☐ Brief Review of TPM
☐ Review Team Responsibilities
☐ Team Brainstorm Task Opportunities
☐ Team Selects TPM Tasks (Use Selection Criteria)
☐ Team Completes Task Analysis Sheets
☐ Team Completes Time Savings Worksheets
☐ Team Plans Next Meeting (if required)
☐ Team Reminded About TPM Charge Codes
☐ Team Apprised of Implementation Sequence to Come After Task Identification
☐ Team Members Asked to Review Tasks with Crews and Provide Feedback to Team Leader

---

Figure 7-1
TPM Task Analysis Sheet

Division:_____   Department:_____

Functional Area:_____   Date:_____

Task:_____

Work Order Priority:_____ Currently Done By:_____

Will Be Done By:_____

══

1. Task Time (in minutes):_____

2. Task Frequency: Daily ☐   Weekly ☐   Monthly ☐

   Other (Please indicate)_____

3. Safety Considerations:

                       0   5   10

   -Likelihood of Accident Is: |----|----|----|----|----|----|----|----|----|----|

                              Low   Moderate   High

   -Particular Safety Concern(s):_____

   _____

4. Tool Requirements:_____

   _____

5. Supplies Needed:_____

   _____

6. Operator/Mechanic Is Willing: Yes ☐   No ☐

Approvals:_____ _____ _____

Figure 7-2
TPM Time Savings Worksheet
Maintenance-to-Operations Tasks, page 1

Date_____ Operation/Building #_____

Task_____

Work Order Priority_____ Frequency_____

Currently Done By_____ # Persons Assigned_____

Will Be Done By_____ # Persons Assigned_____

Note: Enter times for "Actions/Conditions" which apply.

PROCESS BEFORE TPM

Action/Condition	Time (In Minutes)
1. Problem Identified and Work Order Prepared	_____
2. Work Order In System Until Assigned	_____
3. Mechanic/CSM Travels to Job Site	_____
4. Get Necessary Permits	_____
5. Job Being Done	_____
6. Return Permits & Notify Operations That Job Is Complete	_____
7. Mechanic/CSM Travels to Next Job or Shop	_____

A. Total Equipment Downtime   _____
   (From Items 1 thru 6)

B. Time Involved for Mechanic/CSM   _____
   (Items 3 thru 7 X # Assigned)

Figure 7-2 (continued)
TPM Time Savings Worksheet
Maintenance-to-Operations Tasks, page 2

PROCESS AFTER TPM

Action/Condition   Time (In Minutes)

1. Problem Identified/Operator Gets Tools, Supplies,
   and Necessary Permits   _____

2. Job Being Done   _____

3. Tools and Extra Supplies Replaced   _____

C. Total Equipment Downtime   _____
    (From Items 1 thru 3)

Downtime Savings (Item A minus Item C)   _____

Mechanic/CSM Time Saved (See Item B)   _____

Figure 7-3
TPM Time Savings Worksheet
Operations-to-Maintenance Tasks, page 1

Date_____   Operation/Building #_____

Task_____

Work Order Priority_____   Frequency_____

Currently Done By_____   # Persons Assigned_____

Will Be Done By_____   # Persons Assigned_____

Note: This sheet is used to analyze the time savings associated with support
      tasks which operators usually perform before and after maintenance does
      a repair task.

PROCESS BEFORE TPM

Action/Condition	Time (In Minutes)
1. Mechanic/CSM Locates Operator	_____
2. Mechanic/CSM and Operator Travel to Work Site	_____
3. Operator Does Support Task	_____
4. Operator Returns to Operating Assignment	_____

***************************Mechanic/CSM Does Repair Task*************************

5. Mechanic/CSM Locates Operator	_____
6. Mechanic/CSM and Operator Travel to Work Site	_____
7. Operator Does Support Task	_____
8. Operator Stands By While Mech./CSM Checks Out Repair	_____
9. Operator Returns to Operating Assignment	_____

A. Total Operator Time (Items 2, 3, 4, 6, 7, 8, 9)	_____
B. Total Mechanic/CSM Time, Excluding Task (Items 1, 2, 3, 5, 6, 7)	_____
C. Downtime Due to Interface (Items 1, 2, 5, 6)	_____

Figure 7-3 (continued)
TPM Time Savings Worksheet
Operations-to-Maintenance Tasks, page 2

PROCESS AFTER TPM

Action	Time (In Minutes)

1. Mechanic/CSM Does Support Task Previously
   Done By Operator   _____

*************************Mechanic/CSM Does Repair Task*************************

2. Mechanic/CSM Does Support Task Previously
   Done By Operator   _____

D. Total Operator Time   ___0.00___

E. Total Mechanic/CSM Time, Excluding Task   _____

Operator Time Saved (Item A minus Item D)   _____

Mechanic/CSM Time Saved (Item B minus Item E)   _____

Downtime Saved (Item C)   _____

IV. Summarize and Publish Workshop Results

After your Primary Implementation Team has chosen the proposed TPM tasks, prepare summaries of the work done in the workshop(s), including meeting notes and lists of the tasks and benefits. Develop an initial tool list, and schedule a review meeting with the Area Implementation Steering Team, whose approval will be required for the TPM tasks. Distribute the meeting notes and task lists to the Primary Implementation Team members and the Area Implementation Steering Team.

TPM Coordinator's Check List
Step 9: Summarize and Publish Workshop Results

☐ Summarize Task Lists
- Initial (Mechanic, CSM, Operator, and others)
- Final (Mechanic, CSM, Operator, and others)

☐ Prepare List of Improvement Opportunities (to be used in Step 21)

☐ Summarize Benefits (From Time Saving Worksheets)
- Maintenance Hours Saved (CSM, Mechanic)
- Operator Hours Saved
- Other Service Group Hours Saved
- Downtime Reduction
- Other Expected Savings (Product, Overtime, etc.)

☐ Develop Initial Tool List

☐ Schedule Review Meeting with Area Implementation Steering Team

☐ Prepare TPM Meeting Notes
- Original Task Lists
- Task Selection Criteria
- Final Task Lists
- Task Analysis Sheets and Time Saving Worksheets
- Initial Tool List
- Benefits Summaries

☐ Distribute Meeting Notes
- Primary Implementation Team Members
- Steering Team (with Notice of Review Meeting)
- TPM Staff Coordinator (with Notice of Review Meeting)

►V.   Conduct Review Meeting with Area Implementation Steering Team

At this meeting, review for the Steering Team the results of the workshop. Get their approval for the TPM tasks. Discuss plans for developing training materials, and lead them to identify which personnel will serve as TPM trainers. A TPM trainer should:

- ► Be knowledgeable about maintenance/operations tasks
- ► Be respected by maintenance and operations peers
- ► Work well with others; be a good team player
- ► Be a self starter
- ► Plan and organize well
- ► Have the ability to instruct others
- ► Have the ability to develop/document training materials
- ► Be willing to be an instructor

Once the trainers are identified, be sure the Area Implementation Steering Team is willing to commit the trainers' time for development of the training materials. Encourage the Steering Team to begin thinking about measure development and reinforcement planning.

TPM Coordinator's Check List
Step 10: Conduct Review Meeting with Area Implementation Steering Team

☐ Review the Following:
- Initial Task List
- Task Selection Criteria
- Final Task List
- Sample of Task Analysis Sheets and Time Savings Worksheets
- Tool List
- Expected Benefits
- General Receptivity

☐ Get Area Implementation Steering Team's Approval for TPM Tasks Accepted

☐ Discuss Plans for Developing Training Materials

☐ Identify Trainers (Operations and Maintenance) If Not Already Determined

☐ Get Commitment of Trainers' Time to Develop Training Materials

☐ Schedule Workshop to Develop Training Materials

☐ Encourage Area Implementation Steering Team to Begin Measure Development and Reinforcement Planning

VI. Develop Training Procedures

Please see Figure 7-4 for a flow chart of the TPM Training Process. The development of training procedures will require several meetings as the materials are created and approved.

The TPM Trainers are those employees who will write the lesson plans and train the other TPM participants in doing the TPM tasks. The best way to implement local equipment-specific training is to use the resident expert in the area as the TPM Trainer. A maintenance mechanic who is well-respected in the area should be the person who develops the TPM equipment-specific training for TPM maintenance tasks that will be transferred to operators or E&I (electrical and instrument) mechanics. Similarly, a well-respected operator should be the person who develops the TPM training for TPM operating tasks that will be transferred to general mechanics or E&I mechanics, and a well-respected E&I mechanic should be the person who develops the TPM training for TPM tasks that will be transferred to operators or general mechanics. One big advantage of using resident experts as TPM Trainers (rather than the Training Department) is that, after the training is complete, the Trainers are normally present in the community where the TPM work is being performed. Therefore, if a TPM participant needs help with a TPM task, he or she can go directly to the person who trained him or her and ask questions.

TPM training should be the only assignment for the TPM Trainers while they are developing and delivering the training.

The Trainers function as a team. The TPM Coordinator trains the Trainers to:

+ Develop lesson plans
+ Write lesson plans
+ Teach the TPM participants to perform the TPM tasks
+ Take care of slow learners
+ Reinforce the learning that takes place

Trainers meet together to write the lesson plans. As they write, they show what they have written to the other Trainers and ask, "Do you understand what I have written?" This partnership approach to writing the lesson plans reduces the chance for misunderstanding. The Trainer who has knowledge of the task may be biased because of that knowledge, and the other two trainers are able to help make the plans clear.

Once the lesson plans are developed and approved, the Trainer delivers the training to a group of participants. However, certification takes place with each participant individually. For example, the general mechanic Trainer will tell a group of operators how to do a task. Then the Trainer will demonstrate the task, after which each operator will tell the Trainer how to do the task and then demonstrate it. Next, both Trainer and operator go to the actual work site or to a training location and certify that the operator can do that task. When the operator feels comfortable doing the task, he or she signs the certification form. Then the Trainer signs the certification form when he or she is confident that the operator is competent to perform the task. At this point, certification is complete.

```
┌─────────────────────────────────────────────────────────┐
│                                                           │
│              TPM Coordinator's Check List                 │
│          Step 11: Develop Training Procedures             │
│                                                           │
│  ☐ TPM Staff and/or Primary Implementation Team Leader    │
│    Initiate/Verify Additional Pay for Trainers            │
│  ☐ Review with the Trainers the Tasks Which Will Require Training │
│    Procedures                                             │
│  ☐ TPM Staff Reviews "How to Write Training Procedures" and Forms │
│  ☐ TPM Staff Representative Works with Trainers and Primary │
│    Implementation Team Leader to Prepare Training Procedures │
│  ☐ Primary Implementation Team Leader and TPM Staff Prepare Packets │
│    of Procedures for Distribution to Area Implementation Steering Team │
│    Members                                                │
│  ☐ Primary Implementation Team Leader Schedules Review with Area │
│    Implementation Steering Team                           │
│  ☐ Distribute Packet of Training Procedures to Area Implementation │
│    Steering Team Members for Review                       │
│  ☐ Review Training Procedures with Area Implementation Steering Team │
│                                                           │
└─────────────────────────────────────────────────────────┘
```

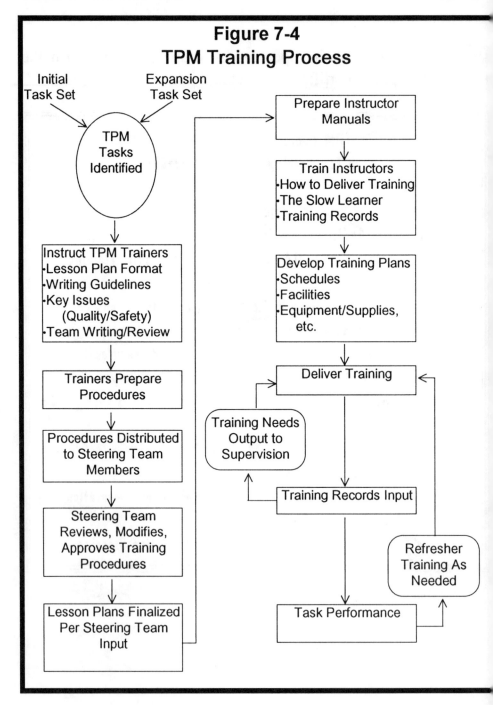

Figure 7-4
TPM Training Process

VII. Arrange for Tools and Supplies

As the training procedures are being developed, arrangements should be made to procure any new tools and supplies which will be needed in performance of TPM tasks.

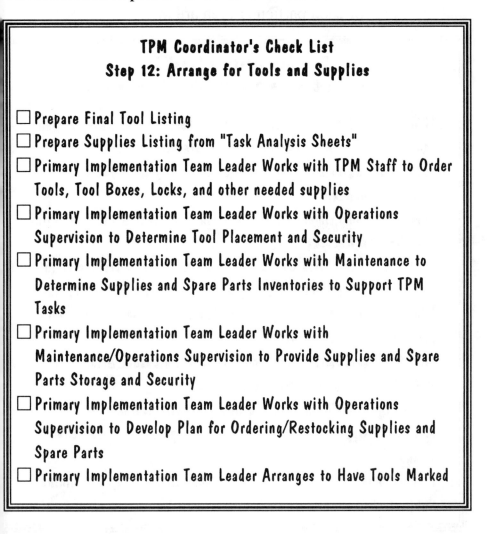

TPM Coordinator's Check List
Step 12: Arrange for Tools and Supplies

☐ Prepare Final Tool Listing
☐ Prepare Supplies Listing from "Task Analysis Sheets"
☐ Primary Implementation Team Leader Works with TPM Staff to Order Tools, Tool Boxes, Locks, and other needed supplies
☐ Primary Implementation Team Leader Works with Operations Supervision to Determine Tool Placement and Security
☐ Primary Implementation Team Leader Works with Maintenance to Determine Supplies and Spare Parts Inventories to Support TPM Tasks
☐ Primary Implementation Team Leader Works with Maintenance/Operations Supervision to Provide Supplies and Spare Parts Storage and Security
☐ Primary Implementation Team Leader Works with Operations Supervision to Develop Plan for Ordering/Restocking Supplies and Spare Parts
☐ Primary Implementation Team Leader Arranges to Have Tools Marked

➤VIII. Develop Area-Specific Training Plan

Each TPM implementation area will have specific needs and training requirements. The TPM Staff and the Primary Implementation Team Leader should work together to be sure that the needs of each particular area are met.

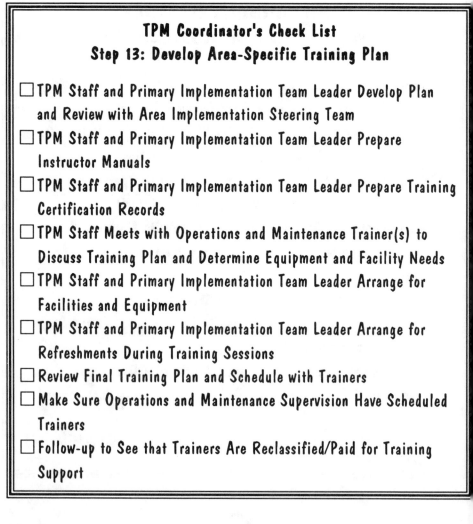

TPM Coordinator's Check List
Step 13: Develop Area-Specific Training Plan

☐ TPM Staff and Primary Implementation Team Leader Develop Plan and Review with Area Implementation Steering Team

☐ TPM Staff and Primary Implementation Team Leader Prepare Instructor Manuals

☐ TPM Staff and Primary Implementation Team Leader Prepare Training Certification Records

☐ TPM Staff Meets with Operations and Maintenance Trainer(s) to Discuss Training Plan and Determine Equipment and Facility Needs

☐ TPM Staff and Primary Implementation Team Leader Arrange for Facilities and Equipment

☐ TPM Staff and Primary Implementation Team Leader Arrange for Refreshments During Training Sessions

☐ Review Final Training Plan and Schedule with Trainers

☐ Make Sure Operations and Maintenance Supervision Have Scheduled Trainers

☐ Follow-up to See that Trainers Are Reclassified/Paid for Training Support

IX. Develop Measures and Plans for Monitoring

The measurement and reporting of TPM data is critical to the success of the program. With accurate data, you will know which TPM tasks are saving money, and you will have concrete results on which to base your reinforcement of TPM personnel. Some of the ways you could handle data collection are:

- ▶ Each TPM performer inputs his or her own data into a computer.
- ▶ Each TPM performer carries around a card on which to list TPM tasks performed and the amount of time used; then, the cards are given to one person at the end of the day to input into a computer.
- ▶ Each TPM performer logs TPM performance on a chart which is kept at the tool and supply area. Periodically, the data from the chart is input into a computer and a report is generated.

Distribution of the data is as important as its collection. Develop a plan for posting the TPM data in a conspicuous place so that all personnel can see the results of the TPM program.

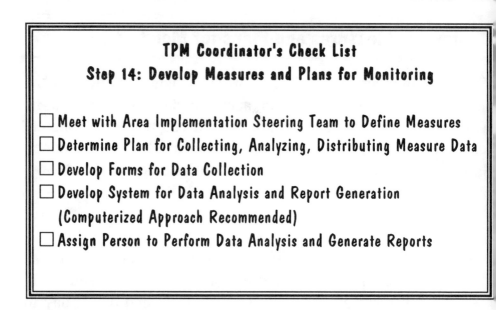

➡️X. Develop Reinforcement Plan

The Area Implementation Steering Team should determine when reinforcement will be given and what type reinforcement will be given. At Tennessee Eastman, we have formal reinforcement "celebrations" at four points in the TPM cycle:

- When all the training for a given TPM implementation area is completed
- When task performance goals and/or results goals are achieved
- When TPM is expanded to include other tasks
- When equipment availability improvements are achieved

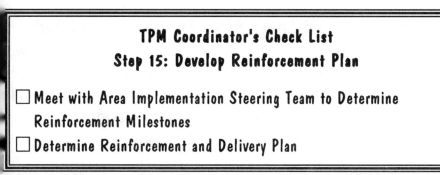

TPM Coordinator's Check List
Step 15: Develop Reinforcement Plan

☐ Meet with Area Implementation Steering Team to Determine Reinforcement Milestones
☐ Determine Reinforcement and Delivery Plan

XI. Deliver Training

As training is delivered, both trainer and trainee must certify that the training is complete and that the trainee is ready to perform the TPM task.

TPM Coordinator's Check List
Step 16: Deliver Training

☐ Trainers Conduct Training Sessions
☐ Trainers/Trainees Certify Task Training on Certification Form
☐ TPM Staff and Primary Implementation Team Leader Monitor Training Sessions to Provide Support and Reinforcement
☐ Primary Implementation Team Leader Collects Certification Forms at End of Training Session; Provides Copy to TPM Staff
☐ Schedule Make-Up Sessions as Needed
☐ Trainers Make Notes on Training Needs or Improvements; Provide These to TPM Staff
☐ Training Records Update

➡XII. Perform Shared Tasks After Training Completed

TPM trainees may begin to perform TPM tasks as soon as they have completed training on a particular task. They will continue to take TPM training on new tasks as they perform those for which they have already received certification.

> **TPM Coordinator's Check List**
> **Step 17: Perform Shared Tasks After Training Completed**
>
> ☐ Operators Begin to Perform Maintenance Tasks
> ☐ Maintenance Personnel Begin to Perform Operations Tasks

➡XIII. Monitor Measures

Once TPM has started, the measures which were determined by the Area Implementation Steering Team must be accurately monitored and reported. Ideally, feedback should be provided weekly. If your system will allow only monthly feedback, develop ways to supplement that with additional weekly data. For example, if Plant Productivity data can be generated only monthly, track department performance weekly. There is a direct relationship between the rate of improvement and the frequency of feedback. At the individual, shift, and department levels, daily feedback is best.

To have the maximum impact, your feedback should be in the form of a graph. The visual display of progress is important. To this end, be sure to choose a scale which will best display small changes in performance. If your baseline is 80% and your goal is 95%, then plot your scale from 75% to 100% rather than from 0% to 100%. This will ensure that small improvements are noticed and continued.

As part of the graphic display, be sure to include the baseline. The baseline should be separated from the subsequent data by a gap and a clear indication (heavy line, for instance) as to when the TPM program began. This allows for accurate analysis of the impact of TPM.

TPM Coordinator's Check List
Step 18: Monitor Measures

☐ Monitor Per Schedule (Weekly Preferred)
☐ Use Graphic Displays
☐ Post Results in Conspicuous Location

XIV. Provide Reinforcement

At Tennessee Eastman, we have used Performance Management as the system to provide reinforcement to TPM participants. Performance Management is based on industrial psychology and deals with goals, feedback, and reinforcement. (For additional information about Performance Management, see Chapter 8.) Performance Management is not the only method of providing reinforcement; if you are in a union atmosphere, negotiations may need to take place in order to pay your people for doing TPM tasks. However, this will add to the total cost of TPM and make it more difficult to justify from a cost savings standpoint.

Whatever your method of "scheduled" reinforcement, you should also use frequent "off-the-cuff" reinforcement -- written praise, oral praise, and pats on the back for those who are participating in TPM and making it work.

TPM Coordinator's Check List
Step 19: Provide Reinforcement

☐ Provide "Off-the-Cuff" Reinforcement
☐ Provide "Scheduled" Reinforcement
☐ Publicize Goals and Progress

➡XV. Expand TPM Application

As a result of monitoring the TPM tasks which have been successfully transferred from maintenance to operations or operations to maintenance, the Primary Implementation Teams will need to reexamine the original task lists and take the following actions:

    (1) Delete a task if the data shows that it does not justify the training, and/or

    (2) Expand TPM application by adding additional tasks.

When the team has identified additional tasks to be added to the TPM lists (by using the Task Analysis Sheets and Time Savings Worksheets), the TPM cycle starts again with Section IV in this chapter (TPM Coordinator's Check List Step 9).

TPM Coordinator's Check List
Step 20: Expand TPM Application

☐ Primary Implementation Team Meets to Identify Additional Opportunities
☐ Expansion to Additional Tasks Follows the TPM Implementation Cycle (start at TPM Coordinator's Step 9)

XVI. Implement Equipment Availability Improvement

This phase of TPM follows the initial TPM implementation and the expansion of TPM to include other tasks. Improving the equipment availability means identifying opportunities to increase the uptime of the equipment, validating the need, and taking steps to pursue the improvement projects to completion. Improving the equipment availability includes, but is not limited to, specific improvement efforts designed to reduce or prevent unscheduled equipment downtime.

Equipment downtime may be caused by equipment failures, product changes (requiring different setups), throughput losses, idle time, minor stoppages, or production of defective material. The equipment availability improvement cycle starts with the reconvening of the Primary Implementation Team. After TPM has been in effect for some period of time, the operators, who now have more ownership of the equipment, and the mechanics, who understand the process better, are able to function as a natural unit team to identify improvement opportunities. They will know which pieces of equipment are the frequent offenders, requiring much reactive and/or preventive maintenance, and, they will be able to think of ways that the TPM task(s) could be eliminated if the equipment were improved.

Using the TPM Equipment Improvements form (Figure 7-5), the Primary Implementation Team should choose the best equipment improvement opportunity and present it to the Area Implementation Steering Team. If the Area Implementation Steering Team agrees that it is a valid opportunity, then the Primary Implementation Team should identify the mechanic, operator, and/or team who is to execute the improvement, propose a solution, and calculate the estimated cost and benefit ratio. After the Area Implementation Steering Team agrees to

150

fund the improvement, the equipment availability team should make the improvements, monitor the progress, and provide feedback to the Primary Implementation Team and the Area Implementation Steering Team.   The Steering Team should decide if the improvement has application in other areas and should provide reinforcement to the Primary Implementation Team for a job well done.

The flow chart in Figure 7-6 illustrates the equipment availability improvement process.

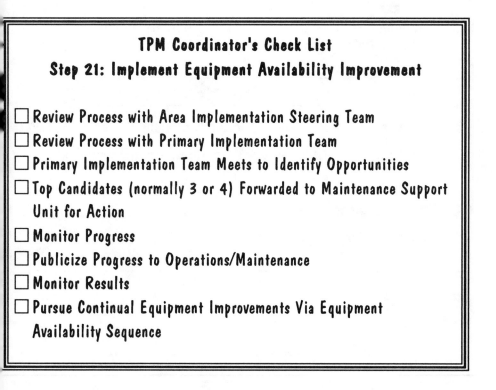

TPM Coordinator's Check List
Step 21: Implement Equipment Availability Improvement

☐ Review Process with Area Implementation Steering Team
☐ Review Process with Primary Implementation Team
☐ Primary Implementation Team Meets to Identify Opportunities
☐ Top Candidates (normally 3 or 4) Forwarded to Maintenance Support Unit for Action
☐ Monitor Progress
☐ Publicize Progress to Operations/Maintenance
☐ Monitor Results
☐ Pursue Continual Equipment Improvements Via Equipment Availability Sequence

Figure 7-5
TPM Equipment Improvements Worksheet, page 1

Date_____

TPM Team_____

Division_____   Dept._____

Building_____

Contact Person_____   Phone_____

IMPROVEMENT OPPORTUNITY

1. Equipment Description/Number_____

_____

2. Equipment Problem (Why is the equipment performing
    unsatisfactorily? Include failure date, if known.)_____

_____

_____

3. How was the improvement opportunity identified? Circle one.

    TPM Workshop   TPM Task Data   Equip. Improvement Workshop

    Other (Please specify)_____

4. Project Sponsor_____

5. Implementation Milestone Dates:_____

_____

_____

_____

_____

_____

_____

Figure 7-5 (continued)
TPM Equipment Improvements Worksheet, page 2

5. Implementation Milestone Dates (continued)_____

    _____

    _____

    _____

    _____

    _____

    _____

    _____

    _____

6. Who is providing solution?_____

7. Completion Date_____

8. Benefits (Estimate dollar value if possible)

    A. Safety_____

    B. TPM Task Reduced_____

    C. Cost Reduced

        1. Maintenance_____

        2. Operations_____

    D. Quality_____

    E. Production_____

    F. Working Conditions_____

9. Other Applications in Plant_____

    _____

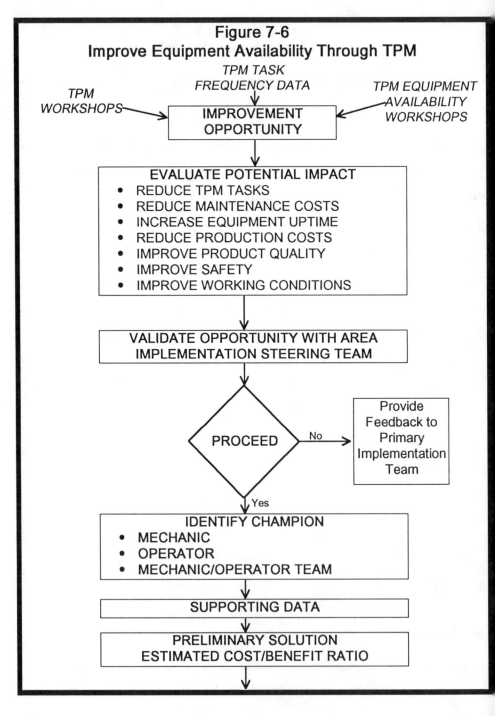

Figure 7-6
Improve Equipment Availability Through TPM

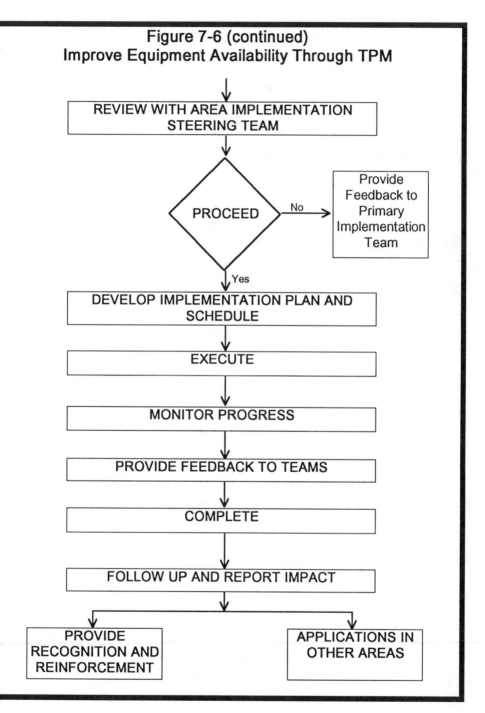

Figure 7-6 (continued)
Improve Equipment Availability Through TPM

REVIEW WITH AREA IMPLEMENTATION STEERING TEAM

PROCEED

No → Provide Feedback to Primary Implementation Team

Yes

DEVELOP IMPLEMENTATION PLAN AND SCHEDULE

EXECUTE

MONITOR PROGRESS

PROVIDE FEEDBACK TO TEAMS

COMPLETE

FOLLOW UP AND REPORT IMPACT

PROVIDE RECOGNITION AND REINFORCEMENT

APPLICATIONS IN OTHER AREAS

XVII. Conclusion

It is our observation that American companies develop many plans but frequently experience difficulty deploying new programs and sustaining their efforts, once begun. Chapters 6 and 7 have suggested a method for implementing TPM throughout an organization. Before you embark on implementing TPM, we suggest that you commit to developing a process similar to the one that has been presented in these chapters. However, remember that TPM success does not depend on good plans; it does depend on deployment, follow-up, reinforcement, and motivating your people to perform. A sustained TPM effort will ultimately save money for your organization.

8   Reinforcement

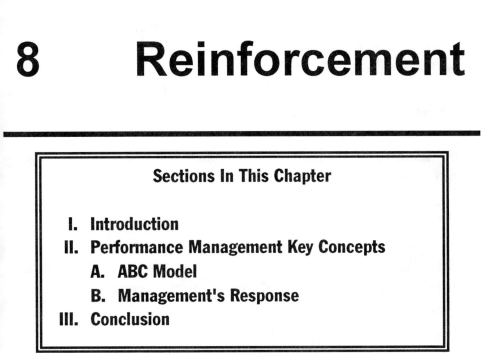

Sections In This Chapter

I. Introduction
II. Performance Management Key Concepts
   A. ABC Model
   B. Management's Response
III. Conclusion

I. Introduction

A key element in any successful TPM implementation is the commitment of the TPM participants to the program. One step in building commitment is to provide reinforcement to the participants as they progress through important stages of the implementation plan. Reinforcement is the positive or negative recognition (feedback) received by employees as a consequence of their job performance. (See section II.B. in this chapter for more complete definitions of positive and negative reinforcement.) TPM works best when it includes goal-setting, a feedback system, and a reinforcement plan. An integral part of the TPM program is a formal recognition program. This could be accomplished in many ways; at Tennessee Eastman, we have used the Performance Management approach. The main thrust of Performance Management is to reinforce the employees for their TPM behaviors and results.

First, identify the behaviors you want to see in your employees (such as cooperatively working together to implement TPM). Next, set goals based on what you want to accomplish with TPM. Finally, give your employees feedback and reinforce that feedback with both tangible, symbolic reinforcements (food, TPM hats, TPM pocket knives) and social (words of praise) reinforcements. The ratio of social reinforcements to tangible reinforcements should be about 4:1.

At TED, a formal recognition is provided when the following milestones are achieved:

- All personnel trained to perform TPM tasks
- Cost reduction goals achieved
- TPM expansion goals achieved (new tasks undertaken)
- TPM task performance goals achieved (total task count)
- Equipment uptime improved

Providing reinforcement/recognition for achieving major milestones acknowledges appreciation for results and provides a necessary catalyst for moving to each successive level in the implementation plan.

158

Without reinforcement, new programs are usually short lived, the resistance to change is often high, the quality of change is spotty, the change is easily extinguished, and employees feel *forced* to change--they do not *want* to change. When you use reinforcement to help implement TPM, the program is more successful, worker behavior changes quickly, you create an atmosphere of enjoyment rather than resistance, the program maintains its momentum, and team capabilities are more fully developed.

The following section briefly explains the key concepts of Performance Management, including reinforcement. It is beyond the scope of this book to fully explain Performance Management; for more information, contact Dr. Aubrey C. Daniels of Aubrey Daniels and Associates, Tucker, Georgia. You may also wish to read *Performance Management,* 3rd edition, Performance Management Publications, Inc., 3531 Habersham at Northlake, Tucker, Georgia, 30084.

II. Performance Management Key Concepts
A. ABC Model

Performance Management theory states that people behave as a result of the consequences or the perceived consequences of their behavior. This theory is explained by the ABC model of why people do what they do. A stands for Antecedents; B for Behavior; C for Consequences. Please see Figure 8-1.

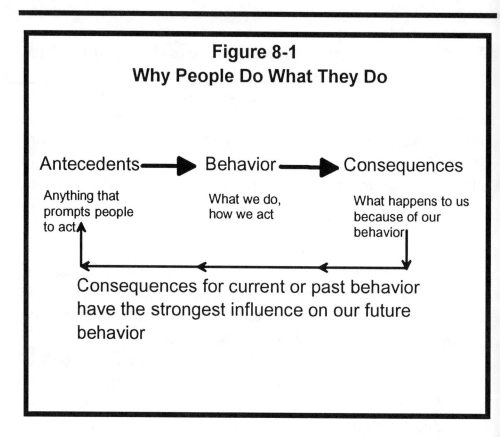

Figure 8-1
Why People Do What They Do

Antecedents ➡ Behavior ➡ Consequences

Anything that prompts people to act.

What we do, how we act

What happens to us because of our behavior

Consequences for current or past behavior have the strongest influence on our future behavior

An **antecedent** is a prompt, cue, stimulus, or reminder that triggers action. Antecedents get people started. Examples of antecedents are objectives, goals, targets, deadlines, priorities, measurement, feedback, training, modeling, policies, past practice, culture, fear, anticipation, meetings, speeches, and rumors. Antecedents communicate information, but they have a short-term effect when used alone. Antecedents are often overused to influence performance because, when they are ineffective, management tends to increase the intensity (i.e., they have more meetings, make more speeches, create more policies, set more deadlines, etc.). When management uses the methods of "retrain, retell, restate, and remind," they have created rework for themselves.

Behavior is an activity that can be observed directly and that the performer is actually doing. Behavior that is followed by positive consequences increases; behavior that is followed by negative consequences decreases.

Consequences can be categorized by *Type*, by the time *When* they will happen, and by the *Probability* that they will happen. See Figure 8-2. The most effective consequences are the PICs (positive, immediate, certain consequences) and the NICs (negative, immediate, certain consequences).

Figure 8-2
Consequences

Type: **P**ositive to the performer
               Negative to the performer

When: **I**mmediately or soon after the behavior occurs
               Future...from one day to several months

Probability: **C**ertain that the consequence will occur
               Uncertain that the consequence will occur

II. Performance Management Key Concepts (continued)
B. Management Responses

Management's job is to manage the consequences. Management is capable of delivering four types of response to employee behavior: Positive Reinforcement, Negative Reinforcement, Punishment, and Extinction. Behavior that is followed by Positive Reinforcement (PICs) or Negative Reinforcement (NICs) increases. Behavior that is followed by Punishment or Extinction decreases.

Positive Reinforcement is feedback that the performer wants (recognition, special opportunities, novelty, acknowledgment, freedoms, tangibles, achievement, anything that meets needs). Any behavior that gets the performers what they want will occur more frequently in the future. Positive reinforcement is the most effective type of reinforcement.

Negative reinforcement is something that the performer dislikes (criticism, crisis, working late, poor review, heat, reprimand, disappointment, failure, embarrassment, anything that is to be avoided). Any behavior that keeps the performer out of uncomfortable situations will occur more often, to a point.

Punishment occurs when the performer receives something which he or she does not like (criticism, denial of privileges, increased controls, getting embarrassed). Punishment will stop behavior.

Extinction occurs when nothing happens (no response, no answer, no interest, no acknowledgment, no questions). The performance just seems to go away.

III. Conclusion

If TPM is to be implemented, company management must agree on how to motivate the employees to "buy into" TPM. Before undertaking a Performance Management approach, a designated person should be properly trained and thus have the knowledge and skills to apply Performance Management techniques.

9 TPM at Tennessee Eastman Division

Sections In This Chapter

I. Introduction

Tennessee Eastman Division (TED) is a division of Eastman Chemical Company (ECC), a subsidiary of Eastman Kodak Company. TED produces and sells over 300 industrial chemicals, 2 basic fibers, and 3 types of plastic. TED employees number 8,110; they are the largest group of the 12,300 ECC employees in Kingsport, Tennessee. TED has approximately 390 buildings on 3,700 acres of land. The 855-acre main plant site includes 37.5 acres of warehouse area under roof and more than 1,100,000 square feet of office space.

In April, 1986, some of our people who had worked in both Operations and Maintenance began to develop a vision of a new work system that we could implement to solve some of our many interface-related problems, delays, and work stoppages. They envisioned a system in which the syndrome of "that's not my job" would be replaced with empowered employees who had stewardship of their processes.

Out of those early meetings came the concept of Total Productive Maintenance -- a partnership between Operations and Maintenance. The primary focus was training operators to perform routine maintenance tasks and training mechanics to perform certain operating tasks.

The TPM program has far exceeded our expectations in terms of realized savings to the company. It is now present in all of TED's operating divisions and in many of the service groups; it has been a story of great success. The demand for reactive maintenance labor has been reduced, and we are able to focus maintenance resources toward reliability improvement.

II. Development of the TPM Program

Figure 9-1 shows the team structure of TPM at TED. At TED, the people who formulated the original concept for TPM (a TPM Committee made up of maintenance superintendents and a representative from Personnel Resources) first studied the "state-of-the-art" methods for breaking down the barriers between craftworkers and operators. They conferred with consultants and other companies and found that, although there were scattered ideas, there was no existing program that fit our organization. What we wanted to do was improve the interface between operators and craftworkers. Therefore, the TPM Committee developed a proposed TPM plan (Figure 9-2). The concepts for the new TPM work system included:

- Empowering operators to perform specified routine maintenance tasks on their equipment.
- Empowering operators to assist mechanics in the repair of equipment when it is down.
- Empowering mechanics to assist operators in the shutdown and start-up of equipment.
- Empowering lower-skilled personnel to perform routine jobs not requiring skilled craftsmen.
- Use of computerized technology to enable operators to calibrate selected instruments.

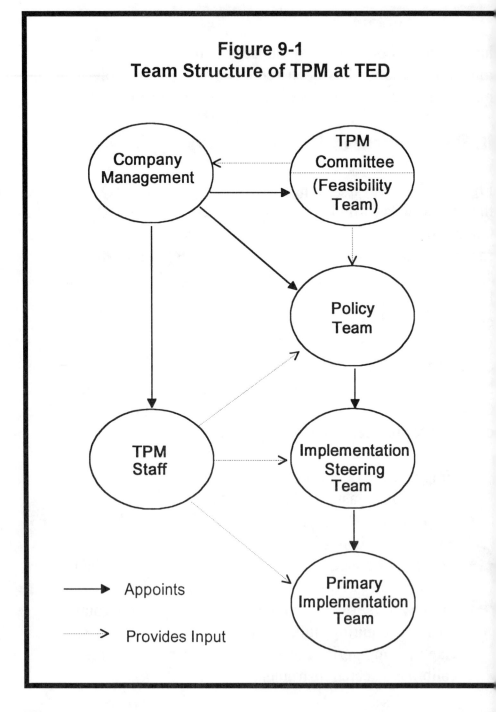

Figure 9-1
Team Structure of TPM at TED

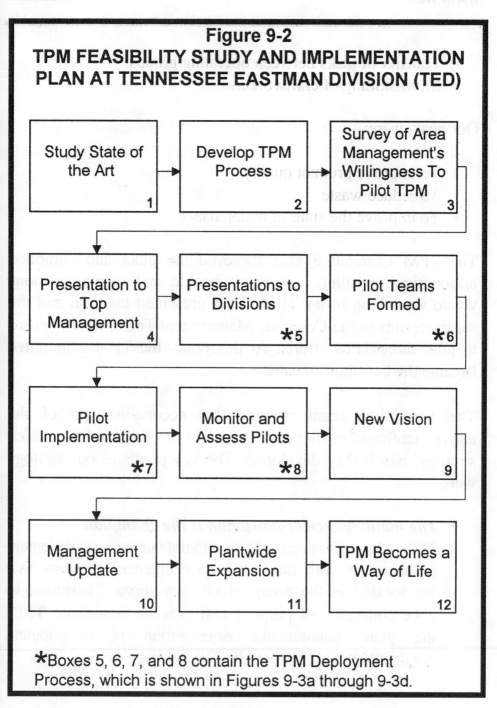

Figure 9-2
TPM FEASIBILITY STUDY AND IMPLEMENTATION PLAN AT TENNESSEE EASTMAN DIVISION (TED)

Study State of the Art **1**	Develop TPM Process **2**	Survey of Area Management's Willingness To Pilot TPM **3**
Presentation to Top Management **4**	Presentations to Divisions **＊5**	Pilot Teams Formed **＊6**
Pilot Implementation **＊7**	Monitor and Assess Pilots **＊8**	New Vision **9**
Management Update **10**	Plantwide Expansion **11**	TPM Becomes a Way of Life **12**

＊Boxes 5, 6, 7, and 8 contain the TPM Deployment Process, which is shown in Figures 9-3a through 9-3d.

- Transfer of tasks between operating groups.
- Multi-skilling of craftworkers.

Our goals were:

- To improve product quality
- To reduce waste
- To improve the state of maintenance

The TPM Committee also surveyed the plant and compiled information revealing how many people and which divisions would be willing to try TPM. They presented the plan and the survey results to the Company Management Team, which agreed to pilot three TPM efforts. At this point, the TPM Committee became the Feasibility Team.

The Feasibility Team realized that accomplishment of the above-mentioned goals would require a detailed implementation strategy, which they developed. The key points of our strategy were:

- *The maintenance organization is the champion.*
  TED has a centralized maintenance management organization with decentralized maintenance groups that are located in the areas which they serve. Therefore, to have constancy of purpose and process throughout TED, the plant maintenance organization is the logical organization to champion the TPM effort.

- ***TPM is a partnership between maintenance and operations.***
  If maintenance people are the champions, their focus must be to establish a partnership symbolized by a handshake between operations and maintenance.

- ***TPM involves teamwork.***
  TPM stresses total teamwork throughout the organization and at all levels of the organization. (For more on teamwork, see Chapter 4, *Team Structure of TPM*.)

- ***Provide teams with a choice.***
  This basically means that operators and mechanics make the decisions. TPM is driven from the bottom up; it is not implemented by management mandate. The people who will be affected by TPM the most are the ones who make the decisions. Also, team decisions are reversible. If a team which has implemented TPM decides at a later date to terminate the program, that is OK. If a task which is approved for transfer does not suit the team after the training and transfer take place, the task can be removed from the list.

- ***Make TPM a structured approach.***
  Any program such as TPM which has the potential to cause much change in the work environment must be handled in an organized, structured fashion, and not haphazardly. The integrity of maintenance and operating procedures must be

maintained during implementation; there should be no losses because a new program is being implemented.

◆ *Pilot before going plantwide.*
Successful pilots in two or three areas will make plantwide implementation more feasible. Knowledge gained from the pilots will be useful in further implementations.

◆ *TPM implementation will be data-based.*
TPM should be based on data so we can measure improvement and reinforce employees for the desired behaviors and results.

◆ *Use performance management to reinforce the people who are involved in TPM.*
We want to use performance management to reinforce behaviors of individuals who make TPM a success. One of these behaviors is "the willingness to do what is needed." It requires the discretionary effort on everyone's part to do what they can to improve and enhance the company's overall productivity, earnings, and profit. Performance management (use of positive and negative feedback) encourages individual effort and continual improvement.

Using these strategies, the Feasibility Team developed the TPM Deployment Process (Figures 9-3a through 9-3d).

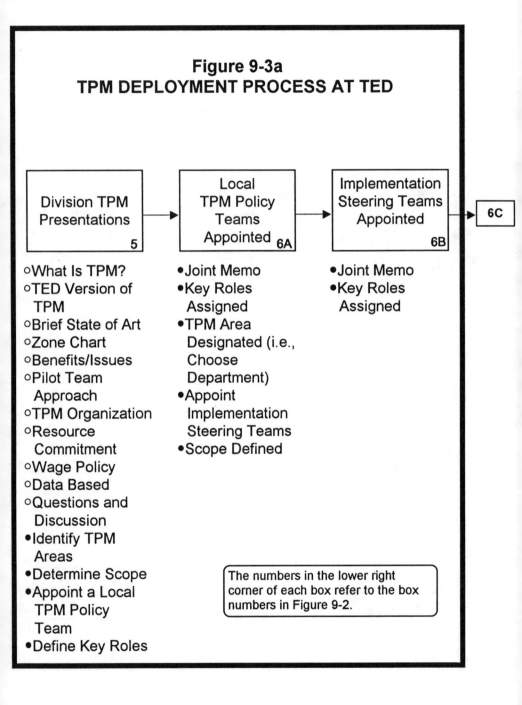

Figure 9-3a
TPM DEPLOYMENT PROCESS AT TED

| Division TPM Presentations **5** | → | Local TPM Policy Teams Appointed **6A** | → | Implementation Steering Teams Appointed **6B** | → | 6C |

○What Is TPM?
○TED Version of TPM
○Brief State of Art
○Zone Chart
○Benefits/Issues
○Pilot Team Approach
○TPM Organization
○Resource Commitment
○Wage Policy
○Data Based
○Questions and Discussion
•Identify TPM Areas
•Determine Scope
•Appoint a Local TPM Policy Team
•Define Key Roles

•Joint Memo
•Key Roles Assigned
•TPM Area Designated (i.e., Choose Department)
•Appoint Implementation Steering Teams
•Scope Defined

•Joint Memo
•Key Roles Assigned

The numbers in the lower right corner of each box refer to the box numbers in Figure 9-2.

173

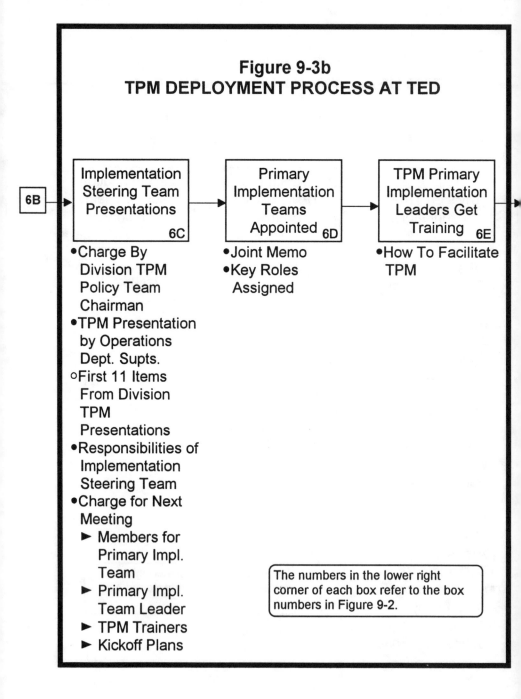

Figure 9-3b
TPM DEPLOYMENT PROCESS AT TED

6B →

| Implementation Steering Team Presentations 6C | Primary Implementation Teams Appointed 6D | TPM Primary Implementation Leaders Get Training 6E |

•Charge By Division TPM Policy Team Chairman
•TPM Presentation by Operations Dept. Supts.
oFirst 11 Items From Division TPM Presentations
•Responsibilities of Implementation Steering Team
•Charge for Next Meeting
► Members for Primary Impl. Team
► Primary Impl. Team Leader
► TPM Trainers
► Kickoff Plans

•Joint Memo
•Key Roles Assigned

•How To Facilitate TPM

The numbers in the lower right corner of each box refer to the box numbers in Figure 9-2.

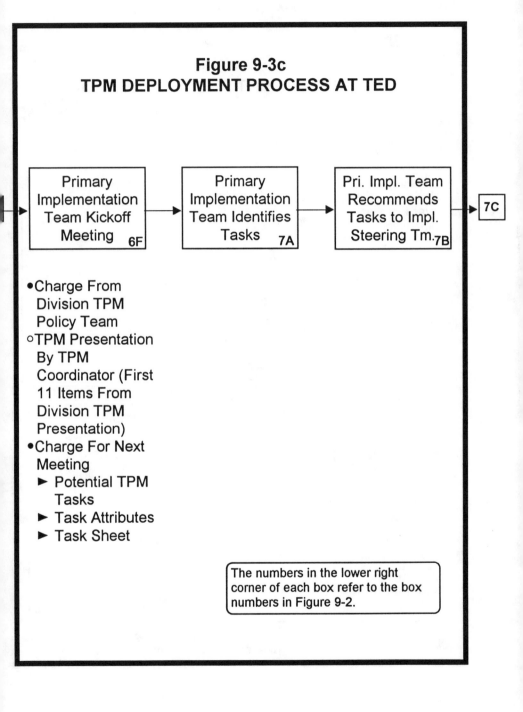

Figure 9-3c
TPM DEPLOYMENT PROCESS AT TED

| Primary Implementation Team Kickoff Meeting **6F** | → | Primary Implementation Team Identifies Tasks **7A** | → | Pri. Impl. Team Recommends Tasks to Impl. Steering Tm. **7B** | → **7C** |

- Charge From Division TPM Policy Team
- ○ TPM Presentation By TPM Coordinator (First 11 Items From Division TPM Presentation)
- Charge For Next Meeting
  - ► Potential TPM Tasks
  - ► Task Attributes
  - ► Task Sheet

The numbers in the lower right corner of each box refer to the box numbers in Figure 9-2.

175

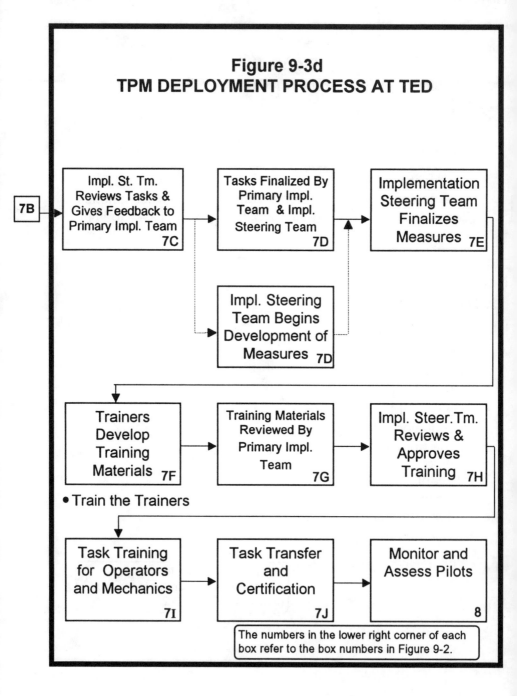

Figure 9-3d
TPM DEPLOYMENT PROCESS AT TED

NOTE: The TPM **Implementation Plan** (Figure 9-2) covers the complete implementation of TPM from start to finish. The TPM **Deployment Process** (Figures 9-3a through 9-3d) refers to the central part of the Plan, starting with TPM's introduction in a particular area (box 5 in Figure 9-2) and ending with the monitoring of task performance in that area after appropriate training has taken place (box 8 in Figure 9-2).

Next, company management asked the Feasibility Team to develop policies pertaining to TPM implementation. Some of the issues they considered were:

- Will we pay for additional skills acquired?
- Will we use Performance Management?
- Will trainers be paid extra?
- Will training be done on regular shifts or on overtime?
- What will our tool policy be?
- What will be our charge codes for expensing time and costs?
- How will we measure success?

III. TPM Pilot Areas Chosen

After the company-wide policies were set, three pilot areas were chosen. In January, 1987, the pilot effort began in three areas -- a production area with a continuous process (Cellulose Esters Division), a production area with a batch process (Organic

Chemicals Division), and a service group (Power and Services Division). Each division had its own Division TPM Policy Team which made decisions about TPM implementation in its particular area. (Some company policies were flexible, allowing for customization in each division.)

Each Division Policy Team appointed an Implementation Steering Team with the following membership:

- Area Engineer in charge of operations
- General Supervisor, Plant Maintenance Division
- Operations Supervisor
- Maintenance Supervisor
- Area Industrial Engineer
- TPM Consultant

The Implementation Steering Team selected the pilot implementation area, appointed the Primary Implementation Team (both leader and members), developed a reinforcement plan, and developed measures and a plan for monitoring the deployment process.

The Primary Implementation Team in each pilot area was made up of the operators and maintenance personnel who would be most affected by TPM implementation. This team was the most important level in TPM implementation. They identified and analyzed the tasks for transfer, developed and performed the training, implemented the task transfer, and monitored the success of the program.

TPM at TED is driven from the bottom up. In our program, operators and mechanics identify the tasks that cause them frequent delays. Then the same people decide if they feel comfortable taking over these tasks. Management applies no pressure to convince them to do specific tasks -- it is totally their decision.

IV. The Three Pilots

A. Cellulose Esters (CE) Division Pilot (Figure 9-4)

Figure 9-4 shows a portion of the first task transfer chart to be used in the CE Division. The five tasks listed on the chart are some of those which were identified by the operators and mechanics in the Film and Fiber Esters area as candidates for transfer. Task number 4, *Isolate a Pump*, is a good example of the savings which materialized as a result of TPM. Before TPM, when a pump bearing needed to be replaced, much communication was required by operators, mechanics, and electricians. When the mechanic arrived to repair the pump, the operator was called to isolate and drain the unit. Then an electrician was called to disconnect power to the motor. After the mechanic repaired the pump, the electrician was called back to reconnect power to the motor, and the operator was called to put the pump back into service. Today, the mechanic does the total job. He is trained to isolate and drain the pump and to electrically disconnect the motor, eliminating delays and craftworker interfaces. Before TPM, this pump repair took about four hours. Today, the mechanic is trained to do the total job in one hour.

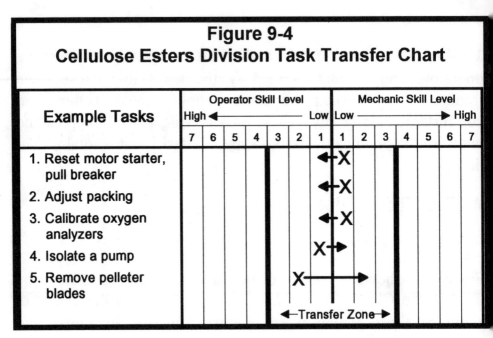

Figure 9-4
Cellulose Esters Division Task Transfer Chart

Example Tasks	Operator Skill Level High ←————— Low							Mechanic Skill Level Low ————→ High						
	7	6	5	4	3	2	1	1	2	3	4	5	6	7
1. Reset motor starter, pull breaker								←X						
2. Adjust packing								←X						
3. Calibrate oxygen analyzers								←X						
4. Isolate a pump							X→							
5. Remove pelleter blades							X	————→						
						←Transfer Zone→								

B. Organic Chemicals Division Pilot (Figure 9-5)

Figure 9-5 shows a portion of the initial task transfer chart for the pilot group in Organic Chemicals. One of their major maintenance problems was rupture disc failure. Before TPM, when a rupture disc failed, the replacement job took from three to four hours to complete. With TPM, the operators are trained, the parts are stored in a cabinet right in the area, and the operator has the proper tools to do the job. He can replace the ruptured disc in about 30 minutes. Delays and costs have been greatly reduced, and uptime of the reactors has been increased by about three hours per occurrence.

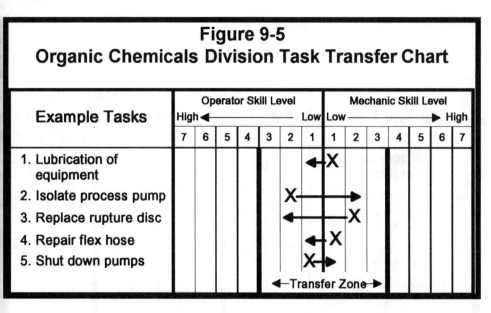

Figure 9-5
Organic Chemicals Division Task Transfer Chart

Example Tasks	Operator Skill Level High ← — Low							Mechanic Skill Level Low — → High						
	7	6	5	4	3	2	1	1	2	3	4	5	6	7
1. Lubrication of equipment								←X						
2. Isolate process pump						X——		——→						
3. Replace rupture disc						←		—X						
4. Repair flex hose								←X						
5. Shut down pumps							X→							
						←Transfer Zone→								

C. Power and Services Division Pilot (Figure 9-6)

Figure 9-6 shows a portion of the initial task transfer chart for the Power and Services Division. One of their big TPM projects involved scrubber shutdowns, a major job which, before TPM, took from five to seven days. Removing the risers, a part of the shutdown, took four mechanics two days to complete. Under TPM, teamwork was used for this task; now we have mechanic and operator working together to complete the riser removal in eight hours. Handling this task and many others with TPM reduced the overall scrubber shutdown time from six days to three and improved uptime on a sold-out product line.

V. Survey of TPM Pilot Groups

At five months into the pilot program, we conducted an attitude survey of the operators and mechanics who were involved in the

Figure 9-6
Power and Services Division Task Transfer Chart

Example Tasks	Operator Skill Level High ◄————— Low							Mechanic Skill Level Low ————► High						
	7	6	5	4	3	2	1	1	2	3	4	5	6	7
1. Install springs/chains on filter racks							◄X							
2. Remove/install guards in air washer fan rooms							◄X							
3. Remove/install risers in scrubbers						◄————————X								
4. Change fan belts, small packaged units						◄————————X								
5. Cut steam off/on for coil repairs						X►►								
						◄—Transfer Zone—►								

TPM pilots. The survey was developed by the operators and mechanics themselves. The result is shown in Figure 9-7. Responses to the right of the neutral line are positive and indicate that 95% of the people felt that TPM was a worthwhile effort.

VI. Decision to Implement TPM Plantwide

The pilots were completed in July, 1987. Because of their success, plantwide expansion of the program at TED was planned. Using input from the three pilots, the TPM staff finalized the TED "TPM Deployment Process" (Figures 9-3a through 9-3d), and plantwide expansion was begun. *However,*

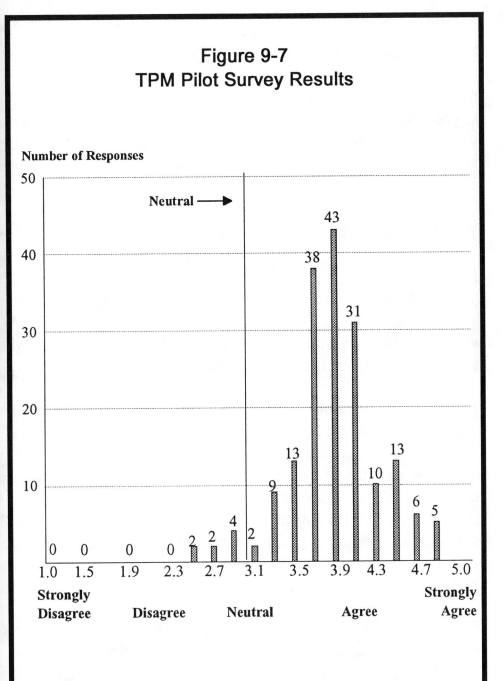

Figure 9-7
TPM Pilot Survey Results

TPM was not dictated as a "must." The new TPM efforts were based on each area's needs and desires to change the way they managed maintenance/operations interfaces. Our philosophy was to grow by success, not by dictate or an ultimatum that everyone was going to have TPM. Each new implementation area had to want the TPM process before any plans were made to implement it there.

VII. Plantwide Implementation of TPM at TED

First, we organized for success by developing a structure which promoted total involvement, including all levels of the organization. During implementation, we had a full-time TPM manager, three full-time consultants, and a plantwide TPM steering team reporting to TED management.

In March, 1990 (about three years into the program), the TPM Staff, which had begun as a part of our Plant Maintenance Division, was transferred to the General Management Staff, reporting directly to the company President. Our President's thinking was that he wanted TPM to be perceived as a company policy, and not a maintenance program. We recommend, for new companies implementing TPM, that the TPM staff be appointed by top management at the beginning. TPM is not a maintenance program.

The culture in which TPM is implemented has a large impact on whether or not it will be successful. Before TPM was piloted, TED had already started studying team management, Statistical

Process Control (SPC), high-performance teams, and performance management. TPM is compatible with all of these and will thrive in an environment where they exist. Why? Because it focuses on team work and other principles incorporated in these management systems.

VIII. Results of TPM at TED

Task turnaround time has shown a 4:1 reduction. In other words, the jobs that once required 4 hours are now completed in 1 hour or less.

The ratio of task skills transferred is, in general, 5:1 -- five transferred from maintenance to operations for every one transferred from operations to maintenance. Even though the operators are taking on more responsibilities than the mechanics, the operators have a positive attitude about TPM. They know that through their efforts to perform routine maintenance tasks, mechanics now have more time to concentrate on the larger and more complicated jobs which improve equipment reliability. Their positive attitude was clearly shown in the survey (Figure 9-7).

From 1987 to 1991, TED realized a 15% reduction in the maintenance which craftworkers were required to perform. In other words, operators are doing 15% of the maintenance work. Several options exist for the very important task of managing this labor reduction. Some options are: (1) have a reduction in work force, (2) control the overtime, (3) make labor available for plant expansions, and (4) improve the state of maintenance. We have been successful in reducing overtime in the TPM areas and providing labor for expansion of the plant facilities. However, our primary focus has been to redirect maintenance labor to improve the state of maintenance, which improves reliability and increases production. Our focus has *not* been to have a work force reduction.

At this point (early 1992) at TED, we have established over 120 TPM teams. Over 3000 interfaces have been identified, and over 2000 of those interface tasks have been approved for transfer. Yearly, over 200,000 individual tasks are performed. That means 200,000 fewer work requests (phone calls, work orders, trips to the shop, etc.) are made. Millions of dollars in savings have been realized.

IX. What We've Learned

Approximately 85% of our efforts have been extremely successful, but about 15 % of our attempts to implement TPM have not been as well received. We list in Section A our observations of reasons for negative TPM experiences; in Section B, those conditions which place obstacles in the path of TPM's success; and in Section C, the attributes which seem to accompany TPM successes.

A. Reasons for Negative TPM Experiences

- One area did not involve the total maintenance organization; they left out shift maintenance.

- One area dictated that TPM would be done.

- In one area, the mechanics trained operators who trained other operators.

- One department put TPM on hold due to their involvement in starting a new work system. When other programs compete for resources, TPM may not succeed.

- Operations and Maintenance middle management were not pro-active in reinforcing the TPM efforts in their areas.

B. Major Obstacles to TPM Implementation

- Adversarial relationships between craftworkers and operators

- Lack of a local TPM champion

- Frequent rotation of employees, either operators and craftworkers, middle management, or top management

- Perception of TPM effort as a maintenance organization program

- Low trust level between craftworkers and their management or operators and their management

- Supervisors or managers left out of the process

- Perceived loss of influence by maintenance

- Perception of "More work, same pay" by operators

C. TPM Key Success Factors

The following conditions are usually present in areas which successfully implement TPM:

► Management's willingness to commit resources

► A centralized, dedicated TPM manager and coordinators

► Dedicated team leaders and trainers

> NOTE: "Dedicated" in this sense means that TPM is the only assignment for these people during the TPM implementation effort.

► Well-defined deployment process

► Team approach with all employees involved

► Tasks identified at the lowest level, not management dictated

► Flexibility in program design

► Pilot approach to tasks

► Emphasis on safety

► Zone concept with task analysis

► Tools and supplies at the job site

► Training developed and done by area mechanics and operators

► Performance management plan to recognize and reinforce behavior and results

► Established vision, mission statement, measures, and improvement plan

X. Vision for the Future

We are now focusing on institutionalizing TPM; i.e., we want to make it a way of life at TED. How will TPM look ten years from now? In ten years, we hope that the phrase "Total Productive Management" does not exist and that the concepts are not perceived as a program. We envision that the concepts will be practiced by all employees as a normal part of doing their jobs.

Glossary

Antecedent - a person, event, thing, or situation that precedes an activity and encourages you to perform that activity.

Area Implementation Steering Team - the group which oversees the specific details of TPM implementation in a particular area. For a complete list of the members and duties of this team, see Chapter 4.

Arrow (➡) - a designation in this book that indicates the responsibilities of a TPM Coordinator.

Baseline Data - data collected before a performance improvement effort that provides a comparison with the data collected after the performance improvement effort. Baseline data helps evaluate the effectiveness of the performance improvement effort.

Benchmark - a reference point of measurement.

Champion - a person who believes that TPM is the best solution for improving a company's interface management and who will actively advocate TPM to other people in the organization.

CLAIR tasks - the five basic low-skill maintenance tasks which operators can easily be trained to perform -- Clean, Lubricate, Adjust, Inspect, Repair.

Company Policy/Steering Team - the group which sets the policies for TPM implementation throughout the organization. For a complete list of the members and duties of this team, see Chapter 4.

Computerized calibration - a method for storing instrument calibrations done in the field; used to track an instrument's reliability and history.

Craft - a job skill which requires specialized training and certification, such as electrical work, mechanical work, control system mechanical work, etc.

Craftworker -   a person who works at a craft, i.e., an electrician, mechanic, etc.

Culture - the overall atmosphere in a company, including the workers' attitudes and feelings about their jobs.

Dedicated - used for one particular purpose. A reactor *dedicated* to acetic acid production is used only to produce acetic acid. A *dedicated* TPM manager has the TPM assignment only, with no other job responsibilities.

Division Policy/Steering Team - the group which sets the policies for TPM implementation throughout a division within an organization. For a complete list of the members and duties of this team, see Chapter 4.

Downtime - the time when equipment is not in use to produce a product.

Empowerment - a management strategy in which employees are given the understanding, knowledge, skills, trust, desire, authority, accountability, and opportunity to manage their jobs.

Equipment reliability - a calculation of the performance of a particular piece of equipment; a measure of how well it produces a given quantity and quality of product.

Equipment availability - a calculation of a piece of equipment's readiness to operate when production is demanded.

Feedback - information on past performance that allows people to change their performance.

High performance team - a team which has gone through a socio-technical redesign to empower employees.

Implementation Steering Team - see Area Implementation Steering Team.

Interface - the point at which people in two different jobs must interact in order to accomplish a task.

Interface management - the process, developed at Tennessee Eastman, which is used to analyze and manage job interfaces and reduce delays created when an individual must depend on another individual to accomplish a task.

Natural unit team - the employees who work together daily to accomplish a unit process.

Off-class - a measure of substandard product. Each company has its own definition.

Performance Management - a systematic, data-oriented approach to managing people at work that relies on positive reinforcement as the major way to maximize performance.

Pilot - a trial effort.

Primary Implementation Team - the group which selects tasks for transfer using TPM and manages the TPM implementation effort in a small work area. For a complete list of the members and duties of this team, see Chapter 4.

Proactive - causing or leading in progress or change.

Quality Management - a management strategy which allows measurement of the degree to which the management process includes customer focus by incorporating the social, technical, and business systems.

Reactive maintenance - maintenance work which is done in response to a breakdown or some other emergency or malfunction.

Reinforcement - a consequence that increases the probability of a behavior occurring in the future.

Shared task zone - an overlap of job tasks among two or more employees so that whoever needs to do the task has the necessary skills.

Skill transfer - the process of one individual properly educating and/or transferring skill knowledge and application to another individual.

SPC (Statistical Process Control) - the use of statistical techniques to attain and maintain the control of a process within its process capability.
State of the art - the way things are today.

Task - a specific job requiring a finite number of steps that is done as part of a person's overall job description. Examples are isolating a pump, resetting a circuit breaker, and changing a fan belt.

Task transfer - the process of transferring primary task responsibilities from one job function to another.

Team management - the process that is used to manage the way teams operate.

Team - a number of persons associated together in work or activity.

TED - Tennessee Eastman Division of Eastman Chemical Company, a division of Eastman Kodak.

TPM (Total Productive Maintenance) - a conscientious, systematic, data-based approach to skill transfer.

Uptime - the time when equipment is producing a product.

Index

About the Author

Bill Maggard was born and raised in the heart of the coal fields in southwest Virginia. He worked as a tool and die designer at Monroe Calculating Machine Company while earning his B.S. degree in Mechanical Engineering from Virginia Polytechnic Institute. Upon graduation, he went to work at Polyscientific Corporation as a manufacturing engineer in aerospace support.

For the past 28 years, Bill has been employed by Tennessee Eastman Division in Kingsport, Tennessee. He has held supervisory positions in research, operations, and maintenance. He presently serves as an Organization Development Consultant and TPM Manager on the General Management Staff of TED. He is a licensed professional engineer in Tennessee.

Over the years, Bill has continued his education by doing graduate studies in industrial engineering and electrical engineering. For the past ten years, his continuing studies have been in the fields of Quality Management, Statistical Process Control, Performance Management, and reliability. He has spoken at many international conferences and has published numerous articles on Total Productive Maintenance.

Bill is a devoted family man, a supporter of his local church, and an active participant in Gideon's International. His hobby is restoring automobiles.